Lilies

Pamela McGeorge

Photographs by Russell McGeorge

FIREFLY BOOKS

A FIREFLY BOOK

Published by Firefly Books Ltd. 2004

First published in 2004 in New Zealand by David Bateman Ltd.,
30 Tarndale Grove, Albany, Auckland, New Zealand

First Printing

Publisher Cataloguing-in-Publication Data (U.S.)

McGeorge, Pamela, 1943-
    Lilies / Pamela McGeorge ; Russell McGeorge, photographer. —1ˢᵗ ed.
[96] p. : col. photos. ; cm.
Includes bibliographical references and index.
Summary: Introductory guide to growing hundreds of species and varieties of lilies, and provides practical advice on how to plant, propagate, cultivate and landscape lilies.
ISBN 1-55297-883-4
ISBN 1-55297-882-6 (pbk.)
1. Lilies. 2. Lilies—Varieties. I. McGeorge, Russell, 1943- . II. Title.
635.9/343 21   SB413.L7.M44   2004

National Library of Canada Cataloguing in Publication

McGeorge, Pamela, 1943-
    Lilies / Pamela McGeorge ; photographs by Russell McGeorge.
Includes bibliographical references and index.
ISBN 1-55297-883-4 (bound).--ISBN 1-55297-882-6 (pbk.)
    1. Lilies. I. McGeorge, Russell, 1943- II. Title.
SB413.L7M34 2004   635.9'343   C2003-905440-3

Published in the United States in 2004 by
Firefly Books (U.S.) Inc.
P.O. Box 1338, Ellicott Station
Buffalo, New York 14205

Published in Canada in 2004 by
Firefly Books Ltd.
3680 Victoria Park Avenue
Toronto, Ontario M2H 3K1

Book design Carpé Diem Publications Ltd
Printed in China through Colorcraft Ltd., HK.

Page 1: *Lilium longiflorum* 'White Elegance'
Page 2: Asiatic hybrids on show
Page 3: Trumpet hybrid seedling

Acknowledgements

Lilies are regal, enchanting flowers. Writing about them and photographing have given us a rare chance to appreciate them in their huge variety. As always, it is the gardeners who make a project like this so enjoyable. To those who have been unstinting in sharing their treasures with us, our grateful thanks and our admiration. We will never forget Ted Alexander's wondrous lilies and his unassuming wealth of knowledge about them. Special thanks are due once again to Keith and Pat Stuart, for their enthusiasm and the pleasure of working in their garden, to Myra Murison, Pauline and Derek Hope, Wendy and David Millichamp and Marianne Johnston, who all gave us the run of their gardens for photography during the flowering season, to Des Paulson and Merle Lepper, who willingly shared their expertise, and to Rosemary McVay for her floristry talent. Several Canadian growers from the prairie provinces also shared their experiences of growing lilies and we are grateful for their help in giving us information about lily behavior in cold climates. Finally, our thanks to Tracey Borgfeldt, who suggested the project and kept us on track during the production process.

Pamela and Russell McGeorge

Contents

Introduction

Lilies. They have been immortalized in art, revered as religious symbols and sought after by plant hunters in dangerous locations. They have been collected, sometimes at great personal cost, shipped "home" to be wondered at, cosseted and in spite of loving care frequently killed. For while they excited the admiration of kings and collectors for centuries, they also gained a reputation with gardeners for being difficult plants – fussy, sulky, prone to a lingering death.

No longer. The image of lilies as garden plants has undergone a transformation – a surprisingly recent one.

Look back through history and it's not hard to find that enthusiasts have been tampering with the genes of tulips, irises, carnations and other so-called florists' flowers for centuries. Hybrids have burst into prominence with the radiance of comets and, in some cases, disappeared just as quickly. Bulbs have been bought and sold for enormous sums. Individual cultivars have created a brief fashion furor – and all before the turn of the 20th century.

But the revolution in lilies started only about 50 years ago, much of it thanks to the efforts of one man, Jan de Graaf, a commercial bulb grower in Oregon. He communicated with lily enthusiasts throughout the world, gathered around him a talented group of horticulturists and together they set about creating hybrids that surpassed in health and beauty any of the lilies that had come before. The result has been a succession of garden plants that has

Opposite: Asiatic hybrid adds a splash of color

Oriental 'Casa Blanca'

caught the imagination of gardeners across Europe, Asia and North America where lily species grow naturally, and in the Southern Hemisphere where they are all introduced.

Interestingly, while the wealth of new hybrids has excited gardeners, it has also led to an enormous increase in the production of lilies sold as a cut flower. Commercial growers raise their crops under cover for 12 months of the year and the blooms are exported around the world to supply a voracious appetite for lilies – whether for bridal bouquets, a simple vase of flowers in the home or for fashionable boutique decorations. A large part of their appeal for florists is their amazing variety. Styles change, colors

7

go in and out of fashion but, whatever the trend, there is a lily for every occasion.

This is similarly the case in the garden. Early in the season I'm entranced by the martagons. I love their Turk's cap flowers and find myself smiling at them. Then a little later it's *Lilium nepalense* that casts its spell. When it is in bloom, I think nothing can match its mysterious allure. But summer continues and I find a glorious tall pink Oriental hybrid to drool over in my garden. The love affair goes on and I haven't even mentioned the bright Asiatics that look so right in today's gardens where growers boldly mix all the fiery hues together.

The sheer diversity of the genus, however, can lead to confusion. This book is for gardeners who love lilies and want to know more about how to look after them and what choices are available. It aims to familiarize readers with the often little-known species and clarify the differences between various divisions in the hybrids.

The book also gives a brief history of how far lilies have come since the days when the Egyptian Pharaohs decreed that carvings of the Madonna lily should decorate their tombs.

A list of suppliers is provided in Appendix II. Many publish their selections or catalogs on the Internet. As with most popular flowers, new lily hybrids are constantly appearing and suppliers can provide the most up-to-date information on which cultivars are available in any given season.

Dainty *Lilium pardalinum* contrasts with Trumpet hybrids.

Hardiness Zone Map

This map has been prepared to agree with a system of plant hardiness zones that have been accepted as an international standard and range from 1 to 11. It shows the minimum winter temperatures that can be expected on average in different regions.

In this book, where a zone number has been given, the number corresponds with a zone shown here. That number indicates the coldest areas in which the particular plant is likely to survive through an average winter.

Note that these are not necessarily the areas in which it will grow best. Because the zone number refers to the minimum temperatures, a plant given zone 7, for example, will obviously grow perfectly well in zone 8, but not in zone 6. Plants grown in a zone considerably higher than the zone with the minimum winter temperature in which they will survive might well grow but they are likely to behave differently. Note also that some readers may find the numbers a little conservative; we felt it best to err on the side of caution.

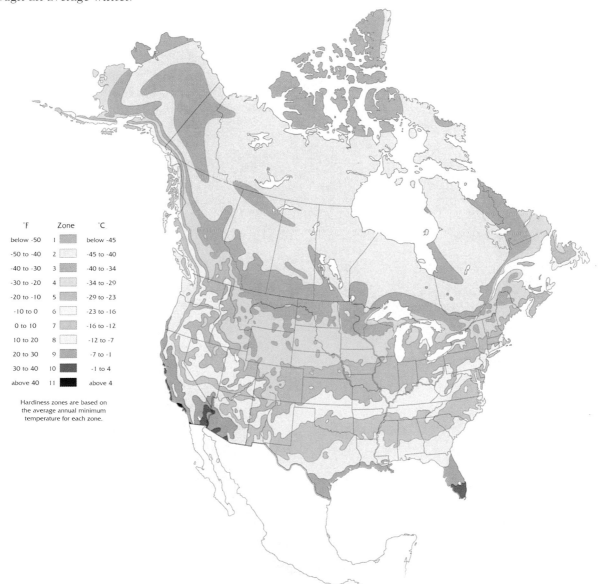

°F	Zone	°C
below -50	1	below -45
-50 to -40	2	-45 to -40
-40 to -30	3	-40 to -34
-30 to -20	4	-34 to -29
-20 to -10	5	-29 to -23
-10 to 0	6	-23 to -16
0 to 10	7	-16 to -12
10 to 20	8	-12 to -7
20 to 30	9	-7 to -1
30 to 40	10	-1 to 4
above 40	11	above 4

Hardiness zones are based on the average annual minimum temperature for each zone.

CHAPTER 1

Lilies Through the Ages

Mention lilies in a group of people and it's possible that everyone will think of a different image, for the word lily is vastly overused. More than 200 widely differing plants are known variously as some kind of lily when referred to by their common name.

The custom could be construed as a compliment, for the word lily has connotations of beauty – though you have to wonder sometimes: toad lily (*Fritillaria meleagris*) seems a particularly unpleasant name for such a distinctive flower. However, it says much about the eternal appeal of the lily that it has maintained its reputation as a symbol of beauty for more than two millennia. Even in our modern world where trends come and go with the speed of electronic transmission, the form of the lily is universally admired.

The Madonna lily, *Lilium candidum*, is one of the oldest domesticated flowers in history. As with other flowers known in ancient times, numerous colorful legends have sprung up around it.

One story tells that the lily sprang from Eve's tears of repentance when she was expelled from the Garden of Eden. Other folklore tells of lilies, unplanted by human hand, that grew spontaneously on the graves of people executed for crimes they did not commit.

In ancient Greek and Roman marriage ceremonies the flowers were placed in the bride's crown as a symbol of fertility. The tombs of the Pharaohs were decorated with designs of white

Opposite: *Lilium candidum*

Oriental 'Egypt'

lilies. Certainly we have been marrying people and burying them with lilies for millennia.

The earliest known record of the existence of the Madonna lily dates from ancient Crete. When the palace of King Minos at Knossos was excavated in the early years of the 20th century, a mural of *L. candidum* was uncovered, the date of the painting probably about 3000 BC.

The Egyptians were familiar with the Madonna lily and imbued it with a mystical significance, regarding it as a symbol of life. This lily is represented on ancient Greek vases dating between 1750 and 1600 BC. Lilies are mentioned in the Bible, though given the indiscriminate use of the name lily, m

Trumpet hybrid of the ryirube group

doubt exists as to which flower was actually meant. The Romans cultivated the lily, seeing it as a symbol of hope, and it is found growing apparently wild in all the countries once included within the bounds of the Roman Empire, although it is thought that the white lily probably went to England in the side panniers of a crusader returning from the Mediterranean. In *The Canterbury Tales*, written in 1387, it merits a mention.

Why is the white lily of old documents .also known as the Madonna lily? The Venerable Bede, a learned monk who lived in England in the seventh century, referred to it in his writings and decreed that it should be the emblem of the Resurrection of the Virgin, a symbol of chastity and innocence – the white petals signifying purity, the golden anthers her soul glowing with heavenly light. Artists picked up on this idea and for centuries depicted the angel Gabriel coming to Mary bearing sprays of lilies in his hand to announce the birth of Christ. It is not surprising that it was often grown in monastery gardens in England. In the 19th century, as more white lilies were grown in England, the name Madonna lily became common.

While few garden writers today are likely to describe flowers in the extravagant terms of the

Venerable Bede, lilies of various types have been appreciated by gardeners for centuries because of their elegant form and their rich perfume. In a garden in summer where lilies are growing among other flowers, visitors will invariably comment first on the lilies.

In his book *Modern Lilies* (1965), Michael Jefferson-Brown reports that the European lily species *Lilium bulbiferum*, *L. croceum*, *L. chalcedonicum* and *L. martagon* were all growing in Britain by the end of the 16th century, and early in the next century the American *L. canadense* appeared there. A slow but steady stream of species followed in the next 200 years, culminating in the introduction of *L. regale* in 1903. This lily was to become one of the most popular on both sides of the Atlantic in the 20th century.

It is not only the flowers of the lily plant that have been sought after for centuries. The bulb was long valued for medicinal purposes and has been endowed with formidable capabilities – few of them proven.

In days gone by, herbalists mashed the bulb of the Madonna lily to treat wounds and, made into an ointment, the bulbs were reputed to take away corns, treat boils and remove the pain and inflammation of burns and scalds.

Gerard, the famous English apothecary, botanist and gardener in the 16th century, said, "Our English white lilie groweth in most gardens of England…" and decreed that, mixed with honey, "[it] gleweth together sinews that be cut asunder. It bringeth the hairs again upon places which have been burned or scalded, if it be mingled with oil or grease…"

The surgeon of Queen Elizabeth I prescribed the juice of the bulb mixed with barley meal for the treatment of dropsy.

Once it was believed that lily petals mixed with honey would produce an ointment to remove wrinkles and smooth the skin. Lily oil from Persia was a costly beauty treatment in the ancient world and if a woman washed with it regularly she was sure to preserve her youthful appearance – certainly less invasive than the surgical beauty treatments of today's world!

Bulbs of both *Lilium lancifolium* and *L. brownii* were traditional ingredients of Chinese medicine. Dried and ground, they were used to make a kind of flour and the indigenous people in the northwestern United States dried the bulbs of native lilies for use as winter food.

In Japan today, bulbs of *Lilium lancifolium* and *L. auratum* are both used as vegetables. In the Kyoto region, lily bulbs are served boiled with a purée of pickled plums as a traditional New Year dish. We may have started using edible flowers to garnish salads but lily bulbs for most of us, I suspect, will stay resolutely in the garden.

CHAPTER 2

What Exactly Are Lilies?

Chances are you've fallen in love with lilies growing in a friend's garden, or you've seen some glorious blooms in a florist's shop and now you want to grow them yourself. Not difficult in theory, but start talking lilies and it's easy to become confused. The genus covers an enormous variety of plants with a huge range in size, flower color, shape and blooming times – not to mention their myriad names and their parentage. Learning to distinguish which is which can make learning a foreign language seem like an easy option. And just to make it more complicated, many of those 200 plants with lily attached to their name are in fact not lilies in botanical terms. Calla lilies, for example, are not part of the lily family. Neither are arum lilies or canna lilies. Even the fabulous Himalayan lily or *Cardiocrinum* is not now considered a true lily, although it does belong to the wider lily family.

Blame it on the botanists. When classifying plants they look carefully not just at the flowers but at all parts of the plant. Seeds, roots and leaves all are assessed before a plant is assigned to a family. Nowadays, DNA testing allows for even more precise analyses and is used to help determine which group a plant finishes up in.

As with people, plant species need names to identify them and link them to other members in the same family. The classification system used today was developed in the 18th century by Swedish botanist Carl Linnaeus (who Latinized his

Opposite: *Cardiocrinum giganteum,* a member of the wider lily family

Lilium longiflorum 'Dutch Glory', a good variety of the Easter lily for gardens in temperate climates

own name). He gave each plant two names in Latin form. The first, that of the genus, is equivalent to our family name. The second is descriptive and serves the same purpose as a person's given name – it denotes a specific individual. Together, these two Latin tags identify a particular species. The system is international.

Botanists continue to develop this system and the entire plant kingdom is divided and subdivided into a multi-branched family tree. As new species are found, or more precise analyses become possible, botanists may rename plants or move them into different families – much to the frustration of everyday gardeners who struggle to learn the names in the first place.

A broad grouping to which a plant belongs is the family. As with humans, there may be other closely related groups – cousins if you like – all members of the same large clan but with distinguishing features that put them in different subgroups or genera.

So the genus *Lilium* belongs to the larger family of Liliaceae and includes the gorgeous Easter lily (*L. longiflorum*), as well as the colorful Asiatics and perfumed Oriental lilies so popular as cut flowers.

Daylilies belong to the family Liliaceae but their genus is *Hemerocallis*. Other genera in the Liliaceae family include the common onion and its relations in the *Allium* genus, *Fritillaria*, some of which resemble lilies closely, and *Aloe* which, at first sight, seem very unlike lilies. Only when you see their tubular, bell-shaped flowers do you start to see why they might be related. Waterlilies are total outsiders, belonging in the family Nymphaeaceae.

Within each genus, there may be one or more species; in the case of *Lilium* there are approximately 100 species and all those multifarious hybrid forms of the flower we know today have originated from these species, which occur widely across North America, Europe, China, Japan and Korea.

An individual plant may be a variety, which, strictly speaking, occurs naturally and is defined by botanists as a taxon below the species level. Alter-natively it may be a cultivar (or clone), which is a variant resulting from human activity. (In common usage the terms cultivar and variety are interchangeable.)

Species will come true to seed – they usually, though not always, have fewer blooms and very often are daintier plants than cultivars, which must be propagated by cuttings or other vegetative means to retain their genetic structure. Many modern cultivars are disease resistant and often come with strong stems and flowers of greater substance and size than those of the species.

The word lily traces its origins to the Greek word *leirion*. From there it passed into the familiar Latin form *Lilium* and so to the English name, lily. In French the word is similar, *lis* or *lys* as in *fleur de lis*, which many of us know as the stylized three-petaled symbol taken by the French King Louis VII as his royal emblem when he embarked on his first crusade. Research indicates, however, that the symbol itself is that of an iris, rather than a lily.

Anatomy of a lily

A lily is a herbaceous perennial growing from a bulb, found in the wild throughout the Northern Hemisphere. Lilies grow near the equator in India but they are also found as far north as Siberia. There are species and hybrids that survive in Canada in temperatures that plunge to -40°F (-40°C) in winter. They grow high on the mountains of Tibet, Western China and Myanmar among low shrubs and rocks; they grow in woodland areas across Europe and in marshy areas in the Eastern United States. They vary in form and size and they have been cherished for centuries.

The bulb

The bulb contains the life force of the plant and, unlike daffodil bulbs, for example, a lily bulb is never

Oriental 'Activa'

Above: A trumpet hybrid with *L. rubellum* and *L. henryi* in its pedigree
Right: 'Bright Star', an Aurelian whose *L. henryi* parentage is obvious

truly dormant and should never be allowed to dry out. Unlike a daffodil bulb also, the lily bulb has no outer, moisture-retaining skin, or tunic, to protect it and it needs to be handled carefully when it is out of the ground. At all times it should look plump and well nourished. Any lily bulb that appears dry or flabby has lost its vitality and is not worth planting.

Size, however, has no bearing on the health of lily bulbs. Depending on the parentage, they can range from little bigger than a marble to as big as a tennis ball.

The bulb consists of a basal plate surmounted by a pyramid of scales, most often tightly packed, occasionally loosely arranged, frequently in a concentric pattern around the stem that emerges from the base. The scales, really modified leaf bases, are easily damaged. They are important assets. They come in many shapes, sizes and colors; they store food reserves for the plant and, detached from the main bulb, will themselves eventually develop into new bulbs.

Most European and Asiatic lilies have concentric bulbs with overlapping scales; this is the most common form among all lilies. These bulbs retain their shape and the daughter bulb develops within the central bulb, close to the base, gradually assuming the same form as the parent. Eventually parent bulb and offspring form a clump of defined

Lilium lancifolium

separate bulbs that needs dividing from time to time. Bulbs of *Lilium regale* or *L. lancifolium* are examples of this type.

There are some species whose bulbs are similar in appearance to those with a concentric form but they increase by sending out underground runners called stolons. During the growing season, the daughter bulb forms at the end of this fleshy stem and it will in turn produce its own flower the following season. The Americans, *Lilium canadense* and *L. michiganense*, reproduce in this fashion, as does *L. superbum*. These bulbs are described as stoloniferous.

The North American species *Lilium pardalinum* and its hybrids have rhizomatous bulbs, which increase in yet another fashion. The original bulb has a wide base and a collection of scales that are

pointed and sitting upright – think of a hedgehog. As the rootstock branches, a new eruption of scales gradually forms a bulb on the extended basal plate and in time a collection of new bulbs exists in close proximity to the parent. Propagation from these offspring bulbs is best achieved by detaching them with a sharp knife, making sure there is a section of the basal plate attached to the scales to prevent them breaking apart.

Several Asian species lilies, including *Lilium duchartrei*, *L. nepalense*, *L. wardii* and *L. lankongense*, often behave in idiosyncratic fashion with stems that wander underground – sometimes as far as 2 ft. (60 cm) – forming bulblets as they go and eventually emerging at some distance from where they were planted before going about their normal growing and flowering habits. These lilies are termed stoloniform or stoloniferous-stemmed.

Lilies usually have two sets of roots – basal roots and stem roots. Some of those extending down from the basal plate have the ability to contract within themselves and thus drag the bulb deeper into the soil or move it sideways. Moving the bulb downward protects it from extremes of weather while helping to anchor the plant more firmly in the soil. Surprisingly, tall lilies often need no staking.

Sideways movement enables the bulb to seek new soil (and therefore fresh nutrients) but provides a trap for unwary gardeners who are over enthusiastic with their spade. Basal roots on established plants can extract moisture from as deeply as 3 ft. (0.9 m)

Bulb Structure and Method of Increase

Stoloniferous bulb as in *Lilium canadense* and *L. superbum*

Rhizomatous bulb as in *Lilium pardalinum*

Concentric bulb – new bulb forms in center – typical of many species and most European and Asiatic lilies

Stoloniferous stem as in *Lilium nepalense*

LA hybrid 'LA Yellow'

helping plants to survive in dry seasons. Individually these roots last about 18 months and are renewed in early fall, after the plants have flowered.

Annual roots form underground, on the flowering stem, just above the bulb – which is why the bulbs of all stem-rooting lilies need to be planted deeply – and these are important feeding roots, contributing significantly to the growth of the plant.

This multi-layered rooting system enables the plant to access nutrients at different levels, a distinct advantage in the wild where leaf litter may enrich the top layers of the habitat.

The stem and leaves

We tend to think of lilies as tall plants with strong stems, but in reality they range in height from merely inches, as in *Lilium nanum*, to sometimes 8 ft. (2.4 m) tall, as in *L. superbum*.

Stems vary in color almost as much as they vary in height. The attractive hybrid 'Tiger Babies' has a dark black-brown stem, repeating the dark freckling of the flowers and contributing to the overall appeal of the whole plant. Stems of the famous 'Casa Blanca', by contrast, blend in with the light green leaves but are so sturdy that even growing to a height of 5–6 ft. (1.5–1.8 m), they need no staking.

The leaves of different species also exhibit considerable variety both in shape and in their arrangement around the stem, and these characteristics are often passed on to their hybrids. They range from the thin and delicate grass-like foliage of *Lilium regale* to the broad, thick boat-shaped leaves of some of the newer polyploid hybrids.

The foliage of *Lilium martagon*, *L. hansonii* and some of the North American lilies is most attractive. Arranged in whorls of pointed, overlapping leaves it looks like a series of elaborate collars spaced at regular intervals up the stem.

On most other lilies the leaves are arranged alternately along the stem and at right angles to it, some so closely that the stem itself is almost hidden.

19

On *Lilium candidum*, however, the leaves are short, closely overlapping and almost upright, creating the appearance of a thick stalk of asparagus.

The lily stems appear above ground in early spring and long before the buds appear they add vertical interest in the garden with their distinctive leaf patterns.

The flowers

Lilies captivate gardeners for a variety of reasons. Some people are seduced by the perfume, others love them for their vibrant colors, but undoubtedly their prime fascination lies in the form of the flowers and in their diversity.

The flowers consist of six stamens and six petals, or more correctly, tepals – three outer sepals and three inner petals – the latter often with

Above: Asiatic 'Rhodos'

nectary furrows leading down to the center of the bloom, exuding nectar to attract insects. These are sometimes a bright color contrasting with the color of the petals. Spotting or freckling on the inner surface of the petals is common; brushmarks, or dark blushes of color on the inside of the petals, are much rarer. Some lilies exhibit papillae on their petals: raised spots, usually of the same color as the main part of the petal, which add texture and character to the individual bloom.

Flowers come in every shade except blue and black, and the color may be uniform or it may be enhanced by a contrasting hue, usually in the center.

There are three basic forms of the lily flower. Turk's cap flowers are pendent (or hanging) and have reflexed petals, some so acutely curled backward that the tips of the petals touch the stem at the base of the flower. This is the typical shape of *Lilium martagon*, *L. lancifolium*, the tiger lily, and many other species from both North America and Asia and is a characteristic passed on to many of their hybrids.

Trumpet flowers are what the casual gardener probably regards as the typical lily flower and the shape, which can vary considerably, seems almost synonymous with rich perfume. The best examples are those two well-known lilies: *Lilium longiflorum*, the Easter/Christmas lily, whose name means long

a. Leaves arranged in whorls as in *Lilium martagon*.
b. Alternate arrangement as in many Asiatic and Oriental lilies.
c. Closed upright arrangement as in *Lilium candidum*.
d. Prolific, fine, grass-like foliage as in *Lilium davidii* and *L. regale*.

Lily Foliage

flower, and *L. regale*, the regal lily, whose trumpet is shorter and flares more widely at the mouth than that of *L. longiflorum*. Bowl-shaped flowers, such as those of *L. auratum*, are more open than trumpets and the petals may reflex slightly. *L. mackliniae*, originally treated as a species of *Nomocharis*, is alone among the lilies in displaying a cup-shaped bloom.

As well as differing in shape, lily flowers have different ideas about presenting their faces to the world. Some look up at the sky; some look out at the world; others hang their heads shyly or peek out from half-hung heads.

The flowers are also arranged in several ways. They may form part of a raceme where the multiple flowers are arranged in series on stalks at the top of the stem; they may form an umbel – as the name implies, a sort of inverted miniature umbrella – where all the flower stalks originate from one point on the stem; or each plant may bear one individual flower per stem.

Flowers of the species tend to be widely spaced; those of some hybrids are closely clustered. It is the arrangement as well as the size of individual blooms that does much to define the character of each lily.

The center of the flower is where all the action takes place. Six stamens emerge from around the female pistil, which contains the ovary at its base. These stamens are composed of slender filaments with anthers delicately balanced at the end and dusted with bright pollen.

This structure can become a feature of the lily flower, especially those of Turk's cap shape, when the filaments are long and extend well beyond the turned back petals.

The anthers on many plants are articulated to give them maximum movement and this helps the wind to disperse their pollen.

The seed capsule

As the petals fall, seeds begin to develop. Once the pod has dried, it splits open to reveal three sections divided by papery tissue, each holding two rows of neatly stacked seeds.

A ripe seed is flat and disk-shaped and there can be more than 100 viable seeds in a single pod. Multiply that by the number of pods produced by each plant and it's easy to see that some varieties of lily are prolific breeders.

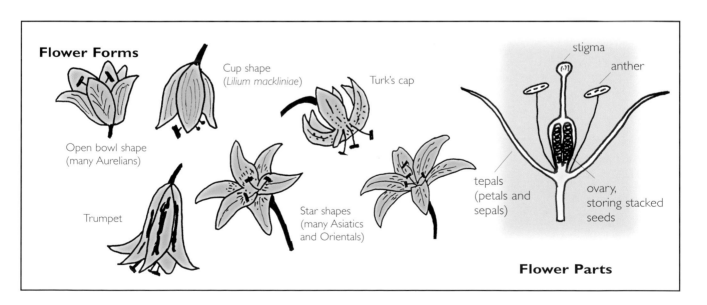

Flower Forms

Open bowl shape (many Aurelians)

Cup shape (*Lilium mackliniae*)

Turk's cap

Trumpet

Star shapes (many Asiatics and Orientals)

stigma

anther

tepals (petals and sepals)

ovary, storing stacked seeds

Flower Parts

CHAPTER 3

Cultivation of Lilies

There was a time when lilies were considered difficult to grow in the home garden. They were often regarded as plants only for the connoisseur who understood the individual needs of chosen species and who was prepared to go to great lengths to provide those special needs – and then sit back and hope they thrived – which often they did not. The problem was dreaded virus disease.

But this started to change with the introduction of *Lilium regale* at the beginning of the 20th century. An attractive plant that proved easy to grow, it led to greater interest in hybridizing. Virus disease, however, still took its toll. Plants would thrive for a few years, then gradually lose vigor and disappear.

However, midway through the century, important progress in hybridizing programs gradually led to the development of disease-resistant lilies that are easy to manage and grow readily from seed. There are now many cultivars that make glorious garden subjects with a minimum of care. However, as with any plants, there are certain basic requirements that need to be met to ensure success. In the chapter on lily species, their particular requirements are discussed individually where appropriate. This chapter deals primarily with the needs of hybrids.

Climate

As a general rule, lilies enjoy cold winters and warm summers but dislike heavy humid weather. Lily growers in the Southern United States and

Left: *Lilium martagon*

A low-growing variety of *Lilium longiflorum* in the perennial garden

Japan have continuing problems with fungus disease because of hot humid summers. Grown in zones 9 and 10, they need shelter from the hot afternoon sun. Where winter temperatures rarely go below 40°F (4.4°C), lily bulbs should be lifted in October and refrigerated for between four to six weeks to imitate a cold winter period, though in zone 10 growers report success with *Lilium longiflorum* without any special chilling treatment.

Of course, climate also affects flowering times and given a warm, wet spring lilies will flower earlier than after a cold dry spring.

Plants growing in shade will frequently produce fewer blooms than those growing in sunny positions. Candidums planted in shade, for example, tend to flower 10–14 days later than those planted in full sun.

Many lily species and cultivars are extremely hardy. John Rempel lives in Winnipeg, Manitoba, where weather conditions are harsh (zone 3). Temperatures range from -31°F (-35°C) in winter, occasionally dropping to -40°F (-40°C), to 95°F (35°C) in summer, with the last frost occurring toward the end of May or as late as the first week in June. Fall frosts arrive about the third week of September. He is a keen lily grower and reports that Asiatics, LA hybrids and martagons are fully hardy in his area without special effort. All are popular with home gardeners and the LA hybrids multiply fast, needing replanting every three to four years.

Choosing a site

"Head in the sun, feet in the shade" is the most common advice referring to the position that lilies like, although they will grow in part shade and the color of the blooms is less likely to bleach where they are protected from searing sunshine.

In the wild, lily species are most often found growing among grass or low shrubs. They seem to like the company of other plants, which in turn provide shade for their roots and, in the case of shrubs, some protection from wind. They do enjoy being well fed, though, and this needs to be kept in mind if they are growing close to trees or hedges. Ground

Above: LA hybrid 'Mt Hood'
Left: 'Nomade', an upward-facing Asiatic hybrid

cover plants such as ajuga are an alternative to mulch and provide some of the same benefits where the climate is not too rigorous.

The soil

Excellent drainage is absolutely essential for success with lilies. Heavy compacted soil is their sworn enemy. Loose soil that allows the basal roots to forage deeply and is gritty or sandy with plenty of humus incorporated into it is ideal. Compost, rotted leaves, composted grass clippings, pine needles, well-rotted manure, sawdust from untreated wood and even seaweed are all suitable sources of humus. These materials themselves retain moisture but by loosening up the soil they also help to ensure good drainage.

Where soil is heavy or waterlogged, it is a good idea to create a raised bed. It needs to be deep enough to accommodate the lily bulbs planted at least 6 in. (15 cm) below the surface, as well as having loose soil beneath the bulb where the roots can develop.

Coarse sand, dolomite and gypsum will help open up clay.

Light, water-permeable soil helps maintain healthy plants. Soggy soil holds too little oxygen, the plants falter and become more susceptible to disease. Damp, warm soils tend to encourage *fusarium*, which destroys the bulbs.

If you are considering using mushroom compost to condition the soil, note that it has a high lime content. Soils vary considerably in their composition, from extreme acidity to extreme alkalinity, the relative levels being expressed as the pH value. A pH of 7 is neutral, a level where many plants are happy. A pH reading of 6.5 and lower indicates soil of acidic composition. The lower the number the higher the level of acidity – so a pH of 2 is extremely acidic, much too acidic for lilies of any type.

A reading above 7 indicates that the soil is more alkaline; the higher the number, the greater the alkalinity. *Lilium candidum* is a lime lover as is its hybrid *L.* x *testaceum*, and failure to grow them can often be ascribed to absence of lime in the soil, but among lilies they are in the minority in liking an alkaline soil. Most prefer a neutral to slightly acid soil.

Asiatics, LA hybrids and longiflorums like a pH of 6–7 – in other words they will tolerate a certain level of lime – while Oriental and other speciosum hybrids do not tolerate lime at all and are happy at 5.5–6.5.

Kits or meters to test the pH of soil are available from most garden centers and are especially useful for determining the composition of the soil in a new garden.

It is possible to change the pH level by adding specific materials to the existing soil; adding a mulch of pine needles, leaf mold or shredded vegetation, for example, will increase the acidity level. Incorporating dolomite or moderate amounts of lime into acidic soil will raise the level of alkalinity.

Lilies thrive in rich soil. Before planting your lily bulbs, incorporate fertilizer into the soil that is high in potash and phosphate. An excess of nitrogen encourages too much soft leafy growth, at the expense of flowers. Well-rotted cow or horse manure and blood or bone meal are all beneficial,

Trumpet hybrids make sensational plants in the garden.

but in warm, humid areas soil that is very rich in animal manures can be a fertile breeding ground for *fusarium*.

Different lilies have different needs and providing the right kind of soil is the first step to successful growing.

Planting

Make sure the bulbs you acquire are fresh. They should be plump, the basal roots should be alive and well and the scales healthy looking. Buy from reputable retail outlets where people have some specialist knowledge of lily bulbs and therefore know how to handle them. If you are unable to plant them immediately, wrap the bulbs in damp moss or damp newspaper to prevent their drying out – but don't forget about them!

All except *Lilium candidum* are best planted in late summer or early fall – this is also the time to move them. They will have time to establish a

strong root system before the soil becomes cold and damp. Candidums need to be moved as soon as they finish flowering.

Take care not to damage the roots when digging up established bulbs for dividing and replanting. In heavy soils or in areas where bugs abide, providing a pocket of coarse sand around each bulb may help to protect it from being munched or succumbing to mold.

All lilies except candidums need to be planted deeply to allow for the formation of stem roots – at least wrist deep makes an easy-to-remember rule. Large bulbs, those of Trumpet hybrids, for example, need as much as 10 in. (25 cm) of soil above the top of the bulb.

If a stake is necessary when the lily is full-grown, it should be stuck in the soil when the bulb is planted, to avoid damaging the bulb at a later date. If you don't like tall, naked stakes overwintering in your garden, a small marker can be used and replaced in spring as the stem grows. It is especially important to mark its original position if the bulb is stoloniferous – an underground explorer.

Lilies enjoy a thick mulch on top of the soil; the same materials as those used to condition the soil are effective. In cold climates where snow is unpredictable, mulch serves as insulation against freeze-thaw cycles over winter, and delays the emergence of frost-tender shoots in early spring – a distinct advantage in areas where late frosts can damage new growth, doing irreparable damage for that season.

Mulch can also provide a ready source of nutrients to be absorbed later by the stem roots, and it retains moisture in spring and summer. Try to ensure that it is weed-free. Bark chips look attractive as mulch but will contribute few nutrients, and bark draws out nitrogen already present in the soil, as does fresh sawdust. Mix it with blood and bone meal to counteract this problem. Gardening without mulch is like sleeping without a comforter!

Single lilies lack impact in a garden so plant several of the same kind in a clump, up to 18 in. (45

Asiatic hybrid 'Update'

cm) apart for large varieties. Overcrowding once the plants have reached full height restricts air circulation and may promote disease.

They take a year or two to attain their full glory and in their second year healthy plants will invariably grow taller and produce more flowers than in their first year of life.

Care

Once the foliage appears in spring, fertilize with either a general, balanced garden fertilizer or with slow-release pellets. An excess of fertilizer, especially one high in nitrogen, can encourage soft, fast growth that will succumb easily to disease.

Replenish the mulch if necessary and make sure your lilies are watered regularly (though still well-drained), especially through spring when they grow fast and up until a few weeks after flowering. A drip system or soaker hose is more effective than overhead watering, which can encourage the development of *botrytis*, especially if leaves and stems remain damp overnight.

Lily roots can reach deep for moisture and will, if necessary, tolerate moderately dry periods in summer. Arthur Evans, who is the director of the North American Lily Society, lives in Arkansas

Above: Commercial growers raise lilies by the thousands under cover.
Left: Asiatic hybrid 'Chetoka'

where rainfall is about 45 in. (114 cm) a year, and he seldom waters his lilies except in severe drought when the plants are trying to grow seedpods. "Frankly," he says, "it's easy to overwater them, especially if they are in tight soil, and growing in level ground."

In terms of overwintering, lily enthusiast John Rempel in Manitoba has devised a useful method for managing his plants. In his beds of Orienpets and especially Trumpets, he uses plastic garbage bags half filled with dry leaves, placed as pillows on top of the tender lilies in early November, just before snowfall. The key to their survival is an early, heavy snow cover, which acts as an insulation blanket keeping the soil underneath relatively stable and warm. He has measured soil temperatures of 28°F (-2°C) under 1 ft. (0.3 m) of snow with air temperatures of -13°F (-25°C).

In the spring, he opens the bags after growth has started and places the contents between the rows to keep moisture in. This can cause problems, however, if there is excessive rainfall in the summer. But summers can also be very dry and he finds a good drip irrigation system is an effective time saver.

If cutting blooms for indoors or merely dead-heading after flowering, leave at least two-thirds of the stem on the plant as it continues nourishing the bulb in readiness for flowering the next season. Unless you plan to propagate it's a good idea to remove the seedpods before seeds start forming; this conserves energy for the bulb. The plants will continue to need watering until all the foliage has turned brown and died, and this is the time to remove the old stems.

Asiatic dwarf varieties

(All grow 24 in./60 cm tall or less)
The following dwarf Asiatics are hardy to zone 3 and will survive -40°F (-40°C) without any winter protection:

'Black Bird'	'Black Jack'
'Buff Pixie'	'Cherised'
'China'	'Crimson Pixie'
'Dawn Patrol'	'Double Creamsickle'
'Happy Thoughts'	'Honey Pink'
'Ladies Choice'	'Lollypop'
'Melissa Jamie'	'Mother Teresa'
'Orange Pixie'	'Silverwood'
'Snow Leopard'	'Stones'

Oriental dwarf varieties

(All grow 24 in./60 cm tall or less)
The following dwarf Orientals are hardy to zone 3:

'Garden Party'	'Matchpoint'
'Miss Birma'	'Mona Lisa'
'Mr. Ed'	'Mr. Sam'
'Rodolpha'	'Tom Pouce'

Even tall lilies grow well in pots, provided they are protected from wind.

Most lilies like to stay put. Do not move them until they become overcrowded with a decline in flowering or start losing vitality. Regale, auratum and speciosum lilies can stay in one place for seven or eight years before being divided. Other varieties can stay in the ground for four or five years before they are lifted, and they should then be moved to a new place in the garden. If this is not possible, be sure to stir up the soil and add some slow-release fertilizer before planting the divided bulbs.

Lilies in containers

Although many lilies are tall plants, they adapt well to container culture. It is important, though, to choose a big container so that the bulb can be planted as deeply as necessary, and there is a good supply of potting mix to nourish it through to flowering.

Often writers recommend planting short varieties in containers. These lilies are suitable for containers because of their short stature, but, like their tall cousins, they will not survive the winter in containers above ground in cold areas.

Lynnette Westfall of Valley K Greenhouses in Edberg, Alberta, reports that the most successful dwarf lilies in her area (zone 2) are those bred on the prairies and brought up from infancy in the rigorous conditions imposed by the climate extremes. The prairie breeders tend to grow and evaluate their lilies over a seven to 10 year period before choosing to register and release them, she says. She highly rates the dwarf varieties from the breeding efforts of Fred Fellner, a hybridizer located near Vermilion, Alberta.

If you're looking for non-dwarf varieties, three Asiatic hybrids can grow together comfortably in a 3.5-pt. (2-l) container. Three bulbs of a large Trumpet variety will need at least a 12-pt. (7-l) container to live happily together for a whole season.

Also note that any tall lilies are vulnerable to strong winds, and a broad-based wooden tub or barrel will be less likely to blow over in windy conditions.

To plant the bulbs, fill the container half full with a free-draining, commercially available potting mix or make up your own with the following mixture: 8 parts fine bark, 2 parts coarse sand (do not use beach sand because of the salt content) and a handful of slow-release fertilizing granules. Do not use garden soil because it will compact quickly, drainage will be impeded and the lilies will not get sufficient moisture to their roots.

Place the bulbs 4–6 in. (10–15 cm) deep and fill the container with the remainder of the mix. Add 1 tbsp. (15 ml) of coated slow-release fertilizer each spring and again before flowering.

Be kind to all your potted lilies in winter. If your area gets frosts, put your potted lilies in a building of some kind to protect them – below-zero conditions will kill them. Keep them in a cool, airy place with strong light, such as a well-ventilated cold greenhouse. In zones 2–4, burying the containers underground makes for good protection.

They will also need protection from excessive rain. Lily bulbs remaining in containers over winter must never be saturated. Although the soil should be kept slightly moist, exposure to constant rain will most likely cause them to rot.

In spring, when the new shoots are approximately 3 in. (7.5 cm) high the plants are ready to enjoy some sun.

Asiatics multiply quickly and will need repotting after two years. LA hybrids, often big, strong plants, will need repotting after one year.

Lilies are big feeders. During the growing season, lilies in containers will need to be fertilized from time to time if slow-release capsules are not incorporated into the mix before the bulb is planted. A feed of tomato fertilizer every two weeks during summer works well.

If leaf color is a rich green then the root system is working effectively at bringing sufficient nutrients to the whole plant. Where foliage is losing color, the plant is probably running out of food. This could happen if a very big bulb is in a small container. Ideally, it should be replanted, but if it's late in the season, add more fertilizer and top up with some fresh potting mix.

As with those planted in the garden, excellent drainage is of maximum importance. The roots should not be allowed to dry out – but don't confuse moist with waterlogged! They can be overwatered. If the lower leaves turn brown and start to fall off, this could be the problem. I mulch containers with an organic mulch to help retain moisture, since drying out is a constant concern. A layer of mulch also helps protect the stem roots just below the surface of the soil.

Beware of aphid attack. Aphids carry virus disease and blithely pass it on. Get rid of the fiends as soon as they appear.

To force plants, move the containers to 64–69°F (18–21°C) when shoots appear, and repot them in the fall.

The advantages of growing lilies this way are numerous. Lilies have a regal air and in containers add instant panache to outside areas. They can be moved into or out of shade or to shelter during high winds. They can be sited in the garden to create an effect, and once the flowering is over they can be banished from sight to die down in obscurity.

CHAPTER 4

The Progenitors: Lily Species

When it comes to growing lilies, we tend to think predominantly of the large flowered hybrids that have been popularized in recent years by their year-round presence in florists' shops. To many of us lilies are bright, in-your-face, mostly star-shaped blooms or luscious, creamy, perfumed trumpets with brilliant yellow pollen.

But there is a wide range of lily species and, as in many genera, they often have a more fragile appearance than their hybrid offspring. The bold flowers of the Asiatics or the Orientals can appear bombastic and gaudy beside the delicate bells of *Lilium canadense* or the mysterious hooded blooms of *L. nepalense*.

The reputation lilies gained in the past as temperamental plants for the home gardener is due in some cases to the difficulty of adapting species to garden situations. Hybridists in recent years have succeeded in producing lilies with improved disease resistance and in so doing have raised the lily's prominence, both as a cut flower for the florist trade and as a gardener's delight. Curiously, though, in an about-face that says more about human nature than that of the plants, many gardeners, having once been seduced by the amazing hybrids, turn to the challenge of growing species.

They are numerous. A few, such as the tiger lily and the Madonna lily, are well known. Some produce flowers like flaring, colored bells; others display the freckled whimsical Turk's cap shape; yet other blooms emerge from long slender buds, the petals

Lilium lancifolium, a hardy garden plant

gradually curling back to expose a deeply colored throat. Most are delicate plants that lend a sense of the exotic to a garden. Some invoke a sense of wonder that nature can produce such exquisite flowers with seemingly careless abandon.

Confusing to the uninitiated is the fact that several separate species are often referred to as the tiger lily, although correctly speaking only *Lilium lancifolium* (formerly *L. tigrinum*) should answer to this common name.

They are tough plants in their native habitat. They have survived for centuries in thin, rocky soil on the Kurile Islands north of Japan, on mountainsides in Nepal, China and Korea, in most of the countries across Central Europe and in bogs and woodland areas of North America. Some are rare and difficult to procure; others grow profusely in their original habitat and have naturalized with ease in their adopted countries.

Opposite: *Lilium nepalense*

'Nippon', an auratum hybrid showing the signature golden rays

The Species Lily Preservation Group, founded in Oakville, Ontario, in 1995, aims to help preserve endangered species and encourage home gardeners to raise them. Members are devoted to the culture, propagation and dissemination of bulbs, pollens and seed of the world's *Lilium* species, with a keen interest in the rare ones. The collection is growing rapidly and the plants are being propagated on the volcanic slopes of Mt. Hood, near Portland, Oregon. Chief grower is Edward McRae, for many years head hybridizer at Oregon Bulb Farms and well-respected lily expert.

An exciting development there is the recent availability of rare and even previously unknown species from China, the likely cradle of *Lilium* evolution, and seedlings are growing now from these recent Chinese imports, including *Lilium rosthornii*, *L. bakerianum*, *L. taliense*, *L. amoenum*, *L. wardii* and *L. speciosum* var. *gloriosoides*, which will both delight the species purists and eventually benefit the hybrid gene pool as well.

In all, close to 100 species have been identified, too many to mention here, but the following selection gives an indication of their variety and highlights those that have been important in the development of modern hybrids.

Left to themselves, plants grow and bloom where evolution has determined they should grow and where conditions suit them, but humans have the need to classify and quantify natural elements. Somehow we find things easier to deal with once lists are made and comparisons can be formed. So botanists over the years have created divisions and groups to sort through the various species according to similarities or differences in flower form, leaf form, bulb habits and geographical distribution. The following well-recognized classification was made by Harold F. Comber and published in 1949. He divided the species into seven categories:

Martagon section:
    L. distichum, *L. hansonii*, *L. martagon*,
    L. medeoloides, *L. tsingtauense*

American section:
  a. *L. bolanderi*, *L. columbianum*, *L. humboldtii*,
      L. kelloggii, *L. rubescens*, *L. washingtonianum*
  b. *L. maritimum*, *L. nevadense*, *L. occidentale*,
      L. pardalinum, *L. parryi*, *L. parvum*, *L. roezlii*
  c. *L. canadense*, *L. grayi*, *L. iridollae*, *L.*
      michauxii, *L. michiganense*, *L. superbum*
  d. *L. catesbaei*, *L. philadelphicum*

Candidum section
(all of which either tolerate or prefer lime soil):
    L. bulbiferum, *L. candidum*, *L. carniolicum*,
    L. chalcedonicum, *L. monadelphum*,
    L. polyphyllum, *L. pomponium*, *L. pyrenaicum*

Oriental section:
    L. alexandrae, *L. auratum*, *L. brownii*,
    L. japonicum, *L. nobilissimum*, *L.rubellum*,
    L. speciosum

Asiatic section:
  a. *L. davidii*, *L. duchartrei*, *L. henryi*,
      L. lancifolium, *L. lankongense*, *L. leichtlinii*,
      L. papilliferum

b. *L. amabile, L. callosum, L. cernuum,*
   L. concolor, L. pumilum
c. *L. bakerianum, L. mackliniae, L. nepalense,*
   L. ochraceum, L. sempervivoideum, L. taliense,
   L. wardii

Trumpet section:
a. *L. leucanthum, L. regale, L. sargentiae,*
   L. sulphureum
b. *L. formosanum, L. longiflorum,*
   L. neilgherrense, L. philippinense,
   L. wallichianum

Dauricum section:
   L. dauricum, L. maculatum

Significant species

Lilium auratum rejoices in the common name of golden-rayed lily of Japan, and with a name like that just has to be gorgeous. Native to Japan, where it grows at the fringes of woods on volcanic hillsides, it was introduced to the West in 1862. It created a sensation at the time because of its large, outward-facing, star-shaped flowers – 10–12 in. (25–30 cm) in diameter with slightly recurving petals – and fragrance, attributes that have been passed on to many of its hybrid children. The "rays" are striking yellow or reddish streaks that radiate out from the throat of the flower to decorate the white petals along with tiny crimson speckles.

Flower stems range from 40–60 in. (102–152 cm) and each one can produce 20–30 blooms. It is not difficult to understand why this is one of the most cherished of garden plants. It looks stunning in late summer or early fall among shrubs and perennials and should thrive if it is planted in well-drained soil with no hint of lime, its feet in the shade and its head in the sun.

Seed germination is delayed hypogeal.

Hardy to zone 6.

Lilium auratum var. *platyphyllum* has larger flowers and fewer speckles and is more vigorous, growing sometimes as tall as 8 ft. (2.4 m). *L. auratum* var. *virginale* has pure white flowers with yellow rays and no spots or speckles.

Lilium pardalinum in the garden

Lilium auratum is one of the most important species in the genus, for along with *L. speciosum* it is the parent of the heavily perfumed, modern Oriental hybrids with large, open-faced flowers. Auratum hybrids that introduce a flush of pink are particularly beautiful.

Lilium bulbiferum is hardy and vigorous. It is known as the fire lily or orange lily for its brilliant orange-red flowers that open as upright blooms with slightly rounded petals, almost cupped in the leaves at the top of the stem. There are two forms, the type that produces bulbils in the leaf axils and gives it its name, and *L. bulbiferum* var. *croceum*, which does not produce the bulbils but which is more common in cultivation. As Edward McRae states in his book *Lilies, A Guide for Growers and Collectors*, the latter is often seen in cottage gardens in England, Ireland and Scotland and is the only lily native to the Netherlands where it was included in paintings by the old masters. Its flowers are more erect and are shallower than the flowers of *Lilium bulbiferum*, which is common in Slovenia, occurs in Italy and grows in the European Alps, where its polished orange flowers may be seen in summer providing flashes of color in hayfields.

The stem of *Lilium bulbiferum* grows 23–47 in. (60–120 cm) tall with scattered narrow, lance-shaped leaves. It prefers acidic soil and the bulbs need lifting and splitting every three to four years to prevent overcrowding, but it is not always easy to find.

First mentioned in books as early as the 16th century, this European lily is mainly important for the part it has played in the development of some early hybrids and therefore in the Asiatic or mid-century hybrids bred by Jan de Graaf in Oregon.

Seed germination is delayed hypogeal.

Hardy to zone 4.

Lilium canadense is often called the Canada lily or meadow lily. Tall (47–80 in./120–203 cm) and delicate looking, with graceful, flaring bell-shaped flowers and whorled sets of leaves, this is a plant that adds elegance to any garden.

It grows wild in damp meadows and thickets from Alabama to Quebec. The flowers in midsummer (often as many as eight per stem but occasionally up to 20) are sparsely spaced, usually yellow but also orange or pinkish red, and are suspended from slender stalks. Hummingbirds like to sip their nectar but they risk being engulfed in the blooms that are nearly 5 in. (13 cm) in diameter.

Raised from seed the plants may take four or five years to bloom. They like sun or light shade and soil that is moist, well-drained and slightly acidic. Unfortunately, cultivated plants are often short-lived. They are susceptible to viruses and growers report that it seems difficult to provide the conditions in which they thrive.

Bulbs are stoloniferous. Seed germination is delayed hypogeal.

Hardy to zone 2.

Lilium candidum, commonly known as the Madonna lily and in the Southern Hemisphere as the Christmas Lily (as is *L. longiflorum*), is one of the best known of the genus. The stems can grow 40–60 in. (102–152 cm) tall and its outward-facing flower with slightly recurved petals is probably the image that most people think of when they think "lily." As many as 20 flowers may be produced on one tall stem. Its Latin name, *candidum*, refers to its dazzling white color, the reason for the Christian Church adopting this flower centuries ago as the symbol of the Virgin Mary and purity.

Although the Madonna lily has been widely cultivated for more than 1,000 years, it is difficult to know exactly where it originated, but the eastern Mediterranean area seems likely. It is found in Afghanistan, Lebanon and Israel.

Prone to *botrytis* and often harboring virus infections, it is safest grown isolated from other lilies, which can either infect it with viruses or be infected by it. It needs to be protected from slugs and snails, which enjoy munching on it.

Unlike other lilies, which like to be planted deeply, *Lilium candidum* should be planted just below the surface of the soil because the stems do not form roots. It is a lime-lover so acidic soil does not suit.

Though it will do well in ordinary garden soil – especially in raised beds – one of the chief causes of disease is planting in low, badly draining soil. It produces the finest flowers when growing in a rich, deep, moist loam, where its roots remain undisturbed for years. No plant dislikes removal or digging near the roots more than this lily. This is the secret of its thriving so well in cottage gardens. It should, therefore, be given a home where it can be left in peace to flourish. Once the plants show signs of deteriorating, they should be dug up, divided and replanted.

The best time for planting, or splitting up and replanting, is when the flowering stem and leaves die down in midsummer. Grown from seeds, plants will be virus-free.

After flowering, this species is typically dormant during hot summers but revives to produce a rosette of leaves when rain comes in fall. Provided it is kept disease-free, it is a vigorous grower and is frost hardy. Seed germination is immediate epigeal and seedlings can flower in their second year.

Hardy to zone 5 where it needs to be mulched over winter.

Confusingly, the so-called peace lily (*Spathiphyllum*), a plant much used indoors, is also frequently known as the Madonna lily, although it is not even a member of the lily family.

Lilium carniolicum is an alpine species that grows in Bosnia, northeastern Italy, Romania and Hungary, and is most common in Slovenia. A mountain plant, it is usually seen on grassy slopes and among rocks but it has been known in gardens since the days of Parkinson, an early English garden writer, who mentioned it in 1629.

The dainty Turk's cap flowers with their velvety orange petals and dark freckles are more tightly reflexed than those of *Lilium chalcedonicum*, giving the bloom a more compact appearance. They are also less brilliant in color. Leaves are pointed and arranged alternately along the stem. Similar to *L. chalcedonicum*, it is, however, a stem rooter and therefore should be planted deeply. In Albania and Greece it occurs as a yellow-flowered variety.

This lily is considered by some as a subspecies of *Lilium pyrenaicum*.

Hardy to zone 5.

Lilium cernuum, known as the nodding lily, is native to Manchuria, Korea and one region in Siberia where it grows in sandy loam, alluvial or rocky soils among grass and shrubs. A relatively low-growing species – 16–24 in. (40–60 cm) – that blooms in mid-July in its natural habitat, it is very cold hardy.

Although the bulbs are small, this species is stem-rooting, which means the bulbs should be planted at least 6 in. (15 cm) deep. The leaves are narrow and grass-like and each stem bears eight or more perfumed flowers in lilac-pink, with petals that curve back deeply, creating a bloom that is almost oval in profile. It's easy to fall in love with this one.

Seed germination is immediate epigeal.

Hardy to zone 2.

Lilium chalcedonicum, the scarlet Turk's cap lily, produces heavily textured, brilliant red flowers in clusters of up to eight or 10 blooms with elegantly reflexed petals, seemingly afloat on longish stalks. It is native to Albania and Greece where it is found on dry hillsides, grassy meadows or in the shade of conifers. It also is abundant about the Lake of Gennesaret on the plains of Galilee and could be the lily mentioned in the Bible. Strong stems can grow up to 36 in. (90 cm) tall with light green leaves that point outward on the lower half of the stem and curl around it as they get closer to the top.

Like *Lilium candidum* this species can be planted shallowly, is happy in a lime soil and also is susceptible to *botrytis*, especially in humid conditions.

Seed germination is epigeal and often delayed.

Hardy to zone 6.

Lilium columbianum grows wild throughout the southern half of British Columbia, is seen as a wildflower on Mt. Rainier and extends as far south as Northern California and eastwards to Idaho. It grows on prairies, in conifer forests and meadows or on cleared sweeps along highways where there is low shrub cover, ranging from sea level up to 5,000 ft. (1,500 m) in altitude.

One of the species to be commonly called the tiger lily, it may have flowers that are orange, pale yellow or near red, of the Turk's cap variety, decorated with purplish dots on the inside. Depending on elevation, flowers appear from late May until July or August. Stems grow 24–60 in. (60–150 cm) tall with leaves arranged in whorls at intervals and the flowers are plentiful.

In the garden these lilies are best raised from seed because they seem not to transplant well and depleting wild stocks is inexcusable. Sow the seeds, in containers, in humus-rich soil in late fall or early winter. Exercise patience. Shoots may not appear until the second season. Transplant to a partly shady, moist site after the small plant has spent a couple of years in a container. The soil must be well-drained and rich in organic matter. Avoid disturbing the bulbs during the growing season.

Traditionally, the bulbs were used for food by the native peoples of the northwestern regions, but, because of their peppery or bitter flavor, were used more as a condiment than a staple. Bulbs were boiled or steamed and sometimes dried for winter use.

Hardy to zone 4.

Lilium concolor, originating in the hills of Central China as well as several areas in Japan, Siberia and Korea, is a dainty lily with wiry stems that support upward-looking, star-shaped, brilliant red flowers that bloom in early to midsummer. Although short-lived, it is easily raised from seed and prefers to grow in full sun so long as its roots are shaded. It has small, erect bulbs, about 1 in. (2.5 cm) in diameter, is stem-rooting, with lance-shaped leaves borne horizontally to the stem and is beautiful as a cut flower. This is another species that has contributed to many hybrids.

Hardy to zone 4.

Lilium dauricum has been grown in Western gardens since the 1780s but comes from the snow-bound regions of Mongolia, Siberia, Northeast China, Japan and Korea. A stem-rooter, it should be planted about 6 in. (15 cm) deep and enjoys full sun.

Flowers appear in early summer, are cup-shaped with flaring petals and are bunched on short stems 12–30 in. (30–75 cm) high; usually vermilion freckled with maroon, they may also appear in softer shades of golden-orange or yellow, as in the variety *Lilium dauricum* 'Lutea'. Dark green leaves are closely scattered up the stem and seed germination is immediate hypogeal.

Hardy to zone 4.

This species played a role in the breeding of the early hybrids *Lilium* x *hollandicum* and *L.* x *maculatum*, both of which in turn played their part in producing the mid-century (more recently named Asian) hybrids. Apricot and yellow forms of *L. dauricum* were used by Jan de Graaf in producing his 'Golden Chalice' strain.

Lilium davidii, named after French missionary and naturalist Père Armand David, is native to Western and northwestern China and is one of the easiest of the Chinese species to grow in almost any fertile soil in reasonable conditions.

The flowers are fragrant, enameled red-orange, with dark spotting and scarlet pollen. They are borne in a long pyramid that can be hung with sometimes up to 40 blooms. While the flowers are

Lilium davidii

gorgeous, the whole plant is attractive. Stems are dark and the leaves are plentiful, dark green, fine and curl downward, each one decorated with a fine, silky tuft of hair where it joins the stem. Flowering in midsummer, it makes a delightful garden species.

Seed germination is immediate epigeal.

A well-known, elegant variety, *Lilium davidii willmottiae* has longer, thicker leaves, the flowers may be even more prolific and the color tends toward orange.

Both plants have been used extensively in hybridizing programs through the years and their genes are present in many enduring Asiatic hybrids, adding the important ingredient of virus tolerance.

Hardy to zone 5.

Lilium duchartrei is a lily that, in a perfect world, I would grow by the dozen, and when it bloomed I would admire it and dream of graceful temples in exotic locations. Sometimes known as the marble martagon lily it is a native of Western China and was introduced into the West by Père Armand David in 1869. It is named after Pierre Etienne Duchartre, a French professor of botany. Recently this species has been found growing at 8,000 ft.

(2,440 m) in northern Sichuan in an open valley of dense shrubs with scattered pines.

Not often found in gardens, it prefers shade where its stems may reach 4–5 ft. (1.2–1.5 m) in height and produce up to 10 flowers with tightly reflexed petals suspended on long stalks and looking like rare Christmas-tree ornaments, startling in white splashed with purple.

Given the propensity of the stems to wander freely below the surface of the soil, forming little bulbs as they go, one bulb will quickly form a colony where it is planted in gritty soil enriched with leaf mold.

Seed germination is immediate epigeal.

Hardy to zone 5.

Lilium formosanum is native to Taiwan where it grows from sea level to more than 9,000 ft. (2,750 m), and is a lily that will do well in warm climates. In subtropical areas, seeds planted in early spring with the resulting seedlings planted out in early summer, will flower in late summer making an attractive addition to the perennial border. But as it tends to lose vigor when mature, fresh plants are necessary to maintain an ongoing display from year to year.

In cold climates it will flower in October and then succumb to frost. New plants can be started from seed each year.

Clusters of fragrant, creamy white, funnel-shaped flowers flaring at the mouth, often flushed purplish pink on the outside, are borne on stems that sometimes reach as high as 10 ft. (3 m). Large pods in fall produce lots of seeds, which can be collected when they are ripe and stored during winter. Plants like well-drained soil and full sun.

'Wilson's White' is a pure white form.

Hardy to zone 8.

Lilium formosanum var. *pricei* is a dwarf form of the species and is also native to Taiwan. Flowers are approximately full size but the stems are short, growing to about 16 in. (40 cm). Also fragrant, these are plants for the rock garden or the front of the border. Mix plenty of organic matter into the soil and make sure that they are well watered.

Lilium grayi is named for Asa Gray, an American botanist who lived in the 19th century and "discovered" this lily. Native to North Carolina, Tennessee and Virginia, it is an uncommon species, closely related to *L. canadense* and displaying a similar elegance. The slender bell-like flowers, with little recurving of the petals, open from long buds and are usually crimson-red in color, spotted in red-purple and tinted orange inside. There may be one per stem or sometimes up to 12. Leaves are narrow, plentiful and arranged in whorls; bulbs are stoloniferous and seed germination is delayed hypogeal.

Hardy to zone 7.

Lilium hansonii is sometimes called the yellow Turk's cap lily or, in an odd mixture of cultural references, the Japanese Turk's cap. Its natural habitat is Korea and Siberia where it is found in pockets of humus on rocky cliffs or in scrub. Harsh winters are no problem.

A stem-rooting species that produces numerous small bulblets, it needs to be planted deeply and

Lilium hansonii

prefers a lightly shaded position with plenty of moist, rich, leaf mold incorporated into its bed.

Leaves are broad and occur in attractive whorls up the stem. It flowers in early summer. Its stems are 40–50 in. (102–125 cm) tall and each one produces between six and 10 marmalade-yellow blooms dotted in brown with swept-back petals resembling a swallow in flight. The petals are thick and strong.

It will thrive in most soils, including limy ones, and is important in the genealogy of lilies for the hybrids that have been produced by crossing it with *Lilium martagon*.

Seed germination is delayed hypogeal.

Hardy to zone 3.

Lilium henryi was named for Dr. Augustine Henry, an Irish plant hunter and forestry professor in China, who "discovered" the plant toward the end of the 19th century. This is an Asian lily, parent with *L. sargentiae* of the Aurelian strains, which were raised by French botanist E. Debray of Orleans and named *aurelianense* by him after the Latin name for his native city. *L. henryi* has contributed widely to many modern hybrids, most notably the 'White Henrys' – bowl-shaped Aurelians with textured, golden-throated white flowers – numerous Trumpet hybrids and the newer Orienpets.

The species is hardy but is more tolerant of warm conditions than some lilies and will grow happily in zone 8. It grows in most soils and does not object to lime. Preferring light shade, it produces enormous bulbs and arching flower stems sometimes reaching to 8 ft. (2.4 m) in height. Lower leaves are dark green, long and broad and it is a lily of stem-rooting habit.

Numerous, large, orange-yellow flowers with emerald-green centers are produced on each stem from mid to late summer. The petals tend to be narrow and somewhat spidery, emphasized by the long filaments bearing the anthers that extend well beyond the lower surface of the flower. One writer describes its shape as somewhere between a Turk's cap and a ten-gallon hat. The bloom has rebel tendencies, with its petals often twisting back at undisciplined angles.

Planted in groups, they look attractive among small shrubs. They increase rapidly from bulblets on the stem, by division of the bulbs and will flower from seed – best sown fresh – in three years.

Hardy to zone 5.

Lilium lancifolium (formerly known as *Lilium tigrinum*) is one of the oldest species in cultivation and is named for its lance-shaped leaves. It is native to Manchuria, China, Japan and Korea where the bulbs have been cooked and eaten for more than 1,000 years. Its signature coloring, which gave it the appealing name of tiger lily, means it can be confused with other species of similar coloring, which erroneously and confusingly are also referred to as tiger lilies. This was the first Asian lily to reach North American shores, arriving in 1804, and it thrives in locations as far apart in distance and climate as Michigan and the Southern States (zone 8).

Above: *Lilium henryi*
Below: A hybrid from *Lilium henryi*

Lilium lancifolium

Although it is sterile and therefore sets no seed, this species is vigorous and easy to propagate because of its habit of producing both bulblets on the stems below the soil surface and bulbils in the leaf axils. Stem bulblets should be planted in fall as soon as they become detached and they will usually flower in their second year.

In cold northern climates both bulblets and bulbils should be potted and grown indoors until the ground thaws and they can be safely planted outside.

These are big feeders, so a mulch of well-rotted cow manure protects the stem roots and nourishes the plant at the same time. Like many lilies they like to be planted deeply – 6–8 in. (15–20 cm) – and have their feet in the shade and their heads in the sun. This lily is a lime-hater.

Use this plant in large drifts in sun, semi-shade or between shrubs. It is a good idea to keep it separate from other lilies because it has the reputation of being susceptible to virus infection, and although rarely seriously affected itself, aphids have no scruples about passing on the disease wherever they suck.

Many varieties are available. Flowers are recurved, with colors varying from bright orange to red, all liberally sprinkled or spread with the signature black dots that often merge to form a dark center. Stems are stiff, set thickly with leaves and may reach 7 ft. (2 m). Flowers appear in clusters of up to 25 nodding blooms from midsummer to early fall. They make good cut flowers.

The tiger lily has played an important part in the development of the modern lily. It is one of the parents of the mid-century hybrids, now called Asiatics, which were developed by Jan de Graaf in Oregon roughly 50 years ago, its inherited vigor an integral component of their success.

Hardy to zone 3.

Lilium lankongense is native to alpine grasslands in Tibet and Yunnan Province in China. It is named for Lankong, where it was found by the French missionary Père Delavay in 1886. Not widely grown in gardens, it's a delicate, intensely fragrant flower with reflexed petals in violet-pink freckled with darker spots. Not unlike *L. duchartrei*, its petals are more pointed and it blooms in mid to late summer, preferring moist, acidic soil, though it is lime tolerant. Stoloniferous by habit, it will not always appear where you thought it was planted. Seed germination is immediate epigeal.

Lilium lankongense crossed with selected Asiatic hybrids has produced some spectacular modern hybrid strains.

Hardy to zone 5.

Lilium leucanthum is native to two provinces in Southern China. The name *leucanthum* means white flowered, and the original lily arrived in England in 1889 but was subsequently lost. *L. leucanthum* var. *centifolium* is native to mountain valleys in Gansu Province and was found in two gardens there by English plant hunter Reginald Farrer in 1914.

It is a tall lily, growing sometimes to 7 ft. (2 m) with fine-textured, glossy, dark green foliage and large, fragrant, creamy trumpets with petals lightly reflexed at the edges and tinged with pale yellow inside and rose-purple coloring on the outside ribs. As the name suggests, each stem bears large numbers of flowers. It blooms in midsummer, will tolerate some lime in the soil and makes a fine cut flower.

Seed germination is immediate epigeal.

Hardy to zone 6.

Lilium leucanthum 'Chloraster' has a bright green stripe down each rib.

Lilium longiflorum 'Dutch Glory'

Lilium longiflorum, the Easter lily of the Northern Hemisphere and the Christmas lily of the Southern Hemisphere, is native to several islands of Southern Japan. Perfumed and pure white with bright golden pollen and a long, slender, trumpet-shaped flower, it is everyone's idea of a traditional lily. This is a concept perpetuated in the United States by the mass production of the bulbs, which are potted, grown in greenhouses and carefully monitored to flower at Easter, when they are sold across North America as cut flowers or indoor container plants.

Easy to cultivate outdoors in temperate climates, *Lilium longiflorum* is frequently sold as a house plant in colder areas. This lily will grow from seed to flower in one season.

Outdoors it prefers partial shade and moist but well-drained soil. Its natural blooming period is midsummer.

Length of stems depends on temperatures, but they may grow as tall as 36 in. (90 cm) with up to 12 flowers on a stem. In cold climates these lilies need mulching in winter. They are hardy outside, with care, in zone 5.

Bulbs for indoor containers should be planted in fall, at least 4 in. (10 cm) deep, in large containers and stored in cool temperatures until winter when they need to be brought inside, watered and fertilized as growth demands.

When choosing a lily to enjoy indoors at Easter time, look for a plant with just one or two open flowers and several buds at various stages of development. Check also that the foliage is abundant and dark green – a sign of general good health. It will require the same care as a lily that you have raised from a bulb.

Place it in bright indirect daylight with daytime temperatures of about 60–65°F (15–18°C) and slightly lower at night – 55–60°F (13–15°C). Avoid placing it near drafts and equally avoid proximity to a source of undue heat or dry air.

Water the plant thoroughly when the soil below the surface feels dry. But avoid overwatering. More

Lilium martagon

indoor plants die from this cause than any other. Plants left in standing water will drown, but placing the container on stones in a saucer filled with water will enable the roots to breathe while maintaining a level of humidity that will encourage flowering. Once the flowers have opened, the plant will need turning every couple of days to prevent it leaning toward the light source.

It is unlikely that your lily will flower a second time indoors but the bulb can be planted in the garden and should resume its natural flowering cycle in the following year.

With over 12 million Easter lilies grown and sold in the United States and Canada each year, their cultivation is an American success story.

In the 19th century most bulbs for commercial production were grown in Bermuda, and for a period the Easter lily adopted the name Bermuda lily. Its popularity as a florist's flower in England even in late Victorian times can be gauged from the following excerpt from *The Garden* of 1895: "It is indeed rare during several months of the year to pass a florist's establishment without seeing its long, pure white blooms exposed for sale either in a cut state or on growing plants in pots."

However, lily stocks in Bermuda eventually became infected with virus, and around the beginning of the 20th century commercial production gradually moved to Japan. Prior to World War II, most of the bulbs in the United States were imported from there.

Pearl Harbor, however, put an end to that trade. The price of lily bulbs skyrocketed and many hobby growers on the U.S. West Coast turned their passion into a business.

Along a small stretch of the Pacific Coast, where California meets Oregon, conditions are perfectly suited to growing this valuable crop. Deep, rich alluvial soil, abundant rainfall and year-round mild temperatures added to the expertise of the growers there have earned this area the title of the "Easter lily capital," and it produces more than 95 percent of the world's potted Easter lilies.

Bulbs are carefully cultivated for three or four years before being shipped to commercial greenhouse growers. Each bulb starts life attached to its mother as a tiny bulblet, growing underground on the parent stem, and is handled numerous times before it is mature enough to be harvested in early to mid fall. This is when commercial-sized bulbs are dug, cleaned, graded, sorted, packed and cooled before being sent to their next destination.

Since the mid-80s, this flower has been an important commercial crop in the Netherlands and its importance is growing in Israel. It is the 'L' partner in the LA hybrids and its genes are present in many hybrids, especially those grown for commercial markets in Japan, the Netherlands and the United States.

Lilium mackliniae is named for Jean Kingdon-Ward, formerly Jean Macklin, wife of the famous plant hunter Frank Kingdon-Ward. He initially found seedpods of the plant in 1946 when he was working for the United States Air Force in Myanmar (formerly Burma), searching for aircraft that had crashed during World War II. He returned with his wife in 1948 and they found hundreds of bulbs in flower in sheltered hollows on a mountainside.

This is a lovely plant that often grows successfully in temperate zones, planted in well-drained acid soil in part shade. However, it is susceptible to viruses so it pays to grow it from seed every few years. Germination is immediate epigeal.

The stem may grow as tall as 4 ft. (1.2 m) in favorable conditions, bearing eight or 10 flowers in early summer. They are bell shaped, gently flaring out at the edges and hang their heads shyly. Kingdon-Ward described the flower as shell pink on the outside and alabaster on the inside. Buds are deep pink.

Hardy to zone 8.

Lilium martagon 'Album'

Lilium martagon is the original Turk's cap lily, its name taken from the Turkish word for a specific kind of turban. A graceful plant, it is sure to win the heart of any flower lover with its perfectly formed flowers suspended from slender stems. It gives its name to a host of hybrids bearing flowers with the typical compact shape and tightly reflexed petals, including the Paisley strain, raised by Jan de Graaf in Oregon.

It is a widespread species, its natural habitat extending from Mongolia in the north to Portugal in the south. One of the oldest species to be cultivated in Britain, it is so widely naturalized there that it has sometimes been considered a native. Martagons are hardy, multiply slowly and can be kept in one location for many years, given well-drained though moist, acidic soil, and a semi-shaded position.

Preferring a cool climate, this species will self-seed where it is happy, though seedlings may take up to seven years to flower. When seeds are planted immediately after harvesting and then undergo a period of cool weather, germination may be relatively fast. Stems may grow as tall as 6 ft. (1.8 m) and bear large numbers of glossy, spotted blooms shyly hanging their heads in a display of color ranging through dusky pinkish red to purplish black. The leaves form attractive whorls at intervals up the stem.

There is also a white form without speckles called *Lilium martagon* 'Album' while hybrids with *L. hansonii* introduce yellow into the color spectrum.

There is a resurgence of interest in the growing of martagons in Canada where there are several good breeders.

Hardy to zone 3.

Lilium michiganense is a widespread species occurring in the wild in North America as a plant of meadows and prairies from Manitoba and Ontario in the north to Tennessee and Arkansas in the

Above left: *Lilium monadelphum*
Left: *Lilium nepalense* before the flowers open completely

south. It is an elegant plant, growing up to 5 ft. (1.5 m) with long leaves occurring usually in whorls along the stem and typically Turk's cap flowers, 3–3.5 in. (7.5–9 cm) across, most often a rich, orange-red freckled heavily with maroon, appearing midsummer. Also stoloniferous in habit, this lily requires similar soil conditions to its close cousin *L. canadense* and thrives in full sun.

Seed germination is delayed hypogeal.

Hardy to zone 2.

Lilium monadelphum is a native of the hills and mountains of the Caucasus and was introduced into Britain in the early 19th century where it became naturalized in a few areas. Its natural habitat includes the margins of woodland, areas of scrub and meadows among thickly growing plants of moderate height. This lily likes to have cool feet with its face in the sun. It enjoys soil rich in leaf mold, will tolerate limy soil and good drainage is necessary.

The bulbs are hardy and long-lived, although transplanting mature bulbs may cause them to sulk unproductively for the first year after being moved. Best to wait until fall before attempting to move them. It sets seed in large quantities and germination is delayed hypogeal.

Dainty bell-shaped flowers with gently recurved petals appear in early summer. They hang their heads modestly, on short stalks and are cheerfully yellow or sometimes pale yellow – or primrose – often lightly speckled with chocolate/purple spots. Frequently the tips of the petals and the base of the bloom are colored wine red.

Planted in clumps these lilies add character to a garden with their stems growing anywhere from 2.5–4 ft. (0.75–1.2 m) tall, profusely clothed with narrow leaves and often carrying up to 10 flowers (although 30 is not unknown).

Hardy to zone 6.

Lilium nepalense, as the name suggests, is native to Nepal where it grows in open scrubland in the

Lilium pardalinum

mountains at 6,600–9,800 ft. (2,000–3,000 m). Also found in Sikkim, Bhutan, India, Myanmar, Tibet and Yunnan Province of China, this lily is heart-stoppingly beautiful. It has to be one of the most evocative flowers I know. To see a stem furnished with its great shrouded flowers that look like a hooded monk when they first open and then gradually turn back their petals as if the wearer is willing to look at the world is a memorable sight.

Its elongated lime-green trumpets with flaring petals and spreading maroon-black hearts suggest eternal mystery.

The bulb is stoloniferous and the stems wander around underground, forming stem bulblets as they go, before emerging and growing perhaps 5 ft. (1.5 m) tall. The flowers appear in early to midsummer and by night are delightfully perfumed.

They detest being wet in fall and winter, a problem that can be avoided by growing them under eaves, under overhanging shrubs or in a greenhouse.

Seed germination is immediate epigeal.

Hardy to zone 5.

Lilium pardalinum, often called the leopard lily, sometimes known as the panther lily, is the flower for gardeners looking for warm-colored blooms to incorporate in today's fiery hued gardens.

It is a dainty plant that grows easily and flowers prolifically, bearing as many as 20 Turk's cap flowers on the stem of a mature plant. They are orange-scarlet in color, shading to gold at the center with purple-brown spots and golden pollen – it's not difficult to understand the origin of the common names!

With each rhizome branching to form a thick mass of bulbs from which, in turn, rises a forest of stems, these lilies quickly form substantial clumps.

Depending on habitat, the plants may grow to 6.5 ft. (2 m) in height. They tolerate an alkaline soil, prefer a moist habitat but abhor continually wet feet and are happy in sun or part shade. They are native to Oregon and California, where they bloom early to midsummer.

Lilium pardalinum is one of the parents of the immensely successful Bellingham hybrids, bred nearly 80 years ago in Bellingham, Washington, by Dr. David Griffiths. Like their parent, these are generous bloomers and are still available today.

In cool conditions, seed germination is hypogeal.
Hardy to zone 3.

Lilium pardalinum giganteum is a strong garden plant with thick strong stems and flowers perhaps slightly larger than the type.

Lilium parryi, the lemon lily, is native to the southwestern United States where it is, increasingly rarely, found growing at 5,900–9,800 ft. (1,800–3,000 m) in California and Arizona. It likes its feet in the shade and its flowers in the sun and will do well where the soil is well-watered but well-drained. The flowers, borne on stems ranging from 2–6 ft. (0.6–1.8 m) tall are funnel-shaped, outward-facing and recurving, a delightful lemon color and have a seductive perfume. A few small purple-brown dots decorate the petals.

Seed germination is hypogeal and not restricted to fall or winter.

It also was involved in the breeding of the Bellingham hybrids.
Hardy to zone 6.

Lilium philadelphicum, in spite of its name, is known across southern Canada, where it blooms in semi-wooded areas in Ontario, British Columbia and the prairies in between, and in nearly all but the Western United States. Commonly called the wood lily, the province of Saskatchewan refers to it as the western red lily and in 1941 adopted it as the provincial flower. In 1935, Mrs. E. D. Flock of Regina, Saskatchewan, suggested that the Regina Natural History Society urge the government to adopt the "prairie lily." A few years later, Mrs. Flock and the Regina Natural History Society spearheaded efforts to protect the red lily, which had become rare. They suggested that it and the sharp-tailed grouse (the provincial bird) be advertised on tourist literature. The lily is also depicted on Saskatchewan's coat of arms, held by a beaver, a national symbol of Canada.

The yellow immaculate lily (*Lilium philadelphicum* var. *andinum* forma *immaculata*) serves as the logo of the Saskatchewan Conservation Data Center. This is a very rare form of western red lily with lemon-yellow flowers that lack dark spots. The yellow immaculate lily is known to occur in fewer than 10 locations in Saskatchewan and a few locations in Manitoba and Alberta. It may also grow on a few plains and in midwest states.

Lilium philadelphicum itself is highly variable, with the stems growing from 18–36 in. (45–90 cm) tall, depending on growing conditions and the genetic make-up of the plant. Although it grows abundantly on roadsides in rural areas, this is not a lily that adapts kindly to growing in gardens. This is a shame because its upward-facing, bowl-shaped, deep red blooms are appealing and somewhat unusual as they appear to form a floating star, with each petal

Lilium pitkinense

seemingly separate from the others because of its long slender shanks. Bulbs are small and stoloniferous in habit. Seed germination is epigeal.

Hardy to zone 3.

Lilium pitkinense was discovered in Sonoma County, California, in 1952, on the property of Sarah Ann Pitkin, hence its name. Declared endangered in 1997, it exists in gardens, planted from seed, which will germinate in late fall in cool conditions. It resembles *L. pardalinum* in appearance; the flowers are Turk's cap in shape, generally a strong red with yellow throats and speckled heavily with dark red dots, blooming in summer.

Hardy to zone 7.

Lilium pumilum, sometimes called the coral lily and formerly known as *L. tenuifolium* for its unusually fine, almost grass-like leaves, has Turk's cap flowers that are fragrant and waxy red. They hang their heads daintily in groups of from one to 20 blooms in a pyramid on slender stems, which normally grow only 12–24 in. (30–60 cm) high, although much taller plants have been found. For this reason it is one of the rare lilies suitable for a rock garden, though a large group of bulbs needs to be planted to make an effective show. It flowers in early summer, although in colder climates flowering may be delayed.

Bulbs are small; it is stem-rooting and will grow readily in well-drained, light, sandy, alkaline soil in full sunshine. Rarely long-lived in the garden,

Lilium regale

it makes up for this by producing plenty of viable seeds, which sometimes produce flowering plants in a year.

Another original inhabitant of cold parts of Asia, it is found in Northern China, Mongolia, Korea and Siberia but will grow happily in the Southern United States in zone 8.

It has been used widely in breeding programs and there is a Yellow Bunting strain that comes true from seed.

Hardy to zone 5.

Lilium pyrenaicum is an early flowering species (late spring to early summer). It is found in Turkey, the Caucasus and its native Pyrenees growing at altitudes of 2,625–7,220 ft. (800–2,200 m) but has naturalized in Britain, growing in hedges and on roadsides, and is very suited to wild gardens. Winter hardy, its stems can grow to about 4 ft. (1.2 m) tall, each bearing between six and 10 compact, nodding, Turk's cap flowers of a vivid yellow freckled with rust, with swept-back, reflexed petals and an unpleasant perfume – not the flowers to bring inside. One grower in Scotland reports that visitors in her garden when *L. pyrenaicum* is blooming inquire whether foxes live there, too! Leaves clothe the stems densely and the bulbs are large. They should be planted at least 6 in. (15 cm) deep.

Seed germination is delayed epigeal.
Hardy to zone 7.

Lilium regale has a very limited natural range along the Min River in northern Sichuan in China and was first introduced in 1903 by E. H. Wilson, the famous English plant hunter. Wilson considered this plant to be one of his most important introductions and, indeed, since its arrival in the West, it has been the leading garden Trumpet lily. So magnificent is this lily that Wilson was moved to write about his view of it in extravagant terms: "There in narrow, semi-arid valleys, down which thunder torrents, and encompassed by mountains composed of mud-shales and granites, whose peaks are clothed with snow eternal, the regal lily has its home. In summer the heat is terrific, in winter the cold is intense, and at all seasons these valleys are subject to sudden and violent wind storms against which neither man nor beast can make headway. There, in June, by the wayside, in rock crevices by the torrent's edge, and high up on the mountainside and precipice, this lily in full bloom greets the weary wayfarer. Not in twos and threes but in hundreds, in thousands, aye in tens of thousands…"

Wilson's discovery was to cost him dearly. His first collection in 1903 rotted in the hold of a ship en route to America and he returned in 1910 to make another collection of the bulbs. Rushing to escape an avalanche on the steep mountainsides where it grew, he fell and his leg was broken in two places. Unfortunately it was not set correctly, leaving him with one leg slightly shorter than the other. For the rest of his life, he suffered from what he called his "lily limp."

Wilson's description of its natural habitat leaves no doubt about conditions the lily likes – good humusy soil, a mulch to protect against late frosts, and full sunshine. It will tolerate limy soil and the bulb prefers to be planted deeply.

It produces copious seeds, which germinate easily with young bulbs producing a single flower in the second or third year. A large, mature bulb may produce up to six large, sweet-scented trumpet flowers in clusters above a crown of leaves, on stems that grow to 5 ft. (1.5 m).

The flower, appearing in midsummer, is colored white inside, pinkish purple on the outside, with anthers and pollen of bright yellow. A pure white form is also available.

Not only appealing to the senses, this lily has been a valuable parent in creating the Trumpet hybrids.

Hardy to zone 5.

Lilium sargentiae is native to Sichuan in Western China where it grows in stony soils among grass and low shrubs. It is another lily collected by E. H. Wilson and like *L. regale* has perfumed, trumpet-shaped blooms. Unlike *L. regale* it is rare in gardens as it succumbs rapidly to virus and *botrytis* and it does not tolerate limy soils.

However, the stunning color of its flowers – pure white on the inside of the petals, a yellow throat, purple-brown on the reverse of the petals with brown pollen on purple anthers – and its willingness to cross with *Lilium regale* to produce *L.* x *imperiale* and with *L. henryi* to produce *L.* x *aurelianense* means that it has become an important progenitor of many modern hybrids, in particular the Trumpet hybrids.

Lilium speciosum, another species from Japan, Taiwan and China where it grows in moist woodlands and on hillsides up to 3,300 ft. (1,000 m), is an important progenitor of the Oriental hybrids. These lilies grow 3–7 ft. (1–2 m) tall, leaves are scattered and leathery in texture, and the blooms, basically white but liberally sprinkled with carmine-red spots, have very reflexed petals and are sweetly perfumed. They bloom from late summer into fall. It lives up to its name, which means "splendid" or "brilliant."

Because of its late flowering season, gardeners in cold areas might prefer to grow this lily in a container where it can be moved to a protected site to avoid early frosts or heavy fall rains.

As with *Lilium auratum* the bulbs are erect, and small bulbs that form on top of the parent bulb can be planted out and new plants will grow from bulb scales. Both species are stem rooting.

Lilium speciosum prefers an acidic soil, rich in humus and likes partial shade. Seed germination is hypogeal. The cultivar 'Rubrum' has carmine-red flowers and is grown in the Netherlands for sale as a cut flower.

Hardy to zone 4.

Lilium sulphureum comes from northern Myanmar and Western China. It is rarely grown as a garden plant, being very susceptible to virus and not hardy in northern climates. Its importance to the gardener lies in its contribution to the Trumpet hybrids. The flowers are large, scented, trumpet-shaped and impressive – of a soft golden color that it has passed on to many of its hybrid children. It is a parent with *L. regale* of an early hybrid *L.* x *sulphurgale*, which itself has been used in hybridizing.

Hardy to zone 6.

Lilium superbum is one of the tallest members of the lily family, capable of reaching more than 10 ft. (3 m). Known as the American Turk's cap lily, it is native to the eastern seaboard in the United States, from Massachusetts to Indiana and south to Alabama. It has been cultivated in English gardens since at least 1738 when John Bartram, a colonial botanist in the early days of European settlement in the United States, sent it to London. This is another graceful plant with a widespread habitat, seeming equally tolerant of moist hilly areas, and bogs and marshes, preferring filtered sun or light shade.

Planted deep in moist, lime-free soil, it does well among small shrubs like rhododendrons that provide a green background for its whorled foliage of long, wide leaves and large hanging blooms with strongly recurved petals. The petals are rich orange-red or yellow, with tips tinted dark red, freckles of brown or reddish hue and a readily identifiable green star in the center. One stem may carry as many as 30 blooms, lasting well for several weeks. Flowering season is midsummer to early fall, and in the garden it is at home with acid-loving shrubs like rhododendrons or azaleas.

Seed germination is delayed hypogeal.

Hardy to zone 3.

Lilium szovitsianum, sometimes called the Caucasian lily, is a close relative of *L. monadelphum* and is now usually regarded by botanists as a subspecies. It was first "discovered" by a Hungarian apothecary with the family name of Szovits. He lived in Odessa and collected plant specimens in the Caucasus and Armenia in the 19th century. *L. szovitsianum* has large, downward-looking flowers of buttery yellow. The main difference between the two plants is the color of the pollen: rust-orange for the Hungarian version, yellow for *L. monadelphum*.

Both these lilies are lime-tolerant and will grow in heavy clay soils although they prefer deep, well-drained, moist soil. They flower early – early to midsummer – and like to rest in the shade for part of the day.

Seed germinates readily but you need to be patient. Leaves won't appear above ground until the second year, and flowering takes a total of five years after sowing.

Hardy to zone 7.

Lilium taliense gives the impression of tiny temple bells suspended in a tall pyramid of delicate color. As with the flowers of *L. duchartrei* or *L. lankongense* the long petals are so reflexed that the tips turn back and touch the base of the flower.

It is a native of limestone soils in mountainous areas of Western China and grows up to 10 ft. (3 m) tall with dark green leaves crowded near the top of the stem. There may be a dozen fragrant flowers per stem but as many as 62 have been reported! Colors of the decorations vary from lemon-gold to green to a dusting of red or maroon speckles, though the petals are always creamy.

Seed germination is epigeal.

Hardy to zone 5.

Lilium tsingtauense has, uniquely for a martagon species, wide open, upright-facing flowers, flamboyantly orange and scented, lightly speckled with maroon. It is a native of Korea and Eastern China where it grows in open forest, scrub and grassland, in a moist shady position. The stem is bare for the lower half and then produces a couple of whorls of leaves with a few single leaves scattered above them, and carries a spike head of one to six flowers. It blooms in early summer on stems up to 18 in. (45 cm) tall and likes a lightly shaded area with well-drained, gritty soil, which has had plenty of leaf mold incorporated into it.

It's not widely available; however, there are specialist nurseries with limited supplies.

Hardy to zone 5.

Lilium wardii is another of the dainty, small flowered species with an attractive Turk's cap flower that is native to southeastern Tibet where it grows in grassy places, scrub and among conifers. Named after Frank Kingdon-Ward, who first collected it in 1924, it grows readily from seed and produces flowers in a soft shade of mauve-pink decorated with deeper pink freckles. Although not very common in cultivation it makes an attractive garden plant, flowering in summer.

The bulb is small and the stem is stoloniferous in habit, wandering underground and producing bulblets as it goes.

Seed germination is immediate epigeal.

Hardy to zone 5.

Above left: *Lilium wardii*
Left: 'Tiger Babies', a hybrid produced by embryo culture, showing its *L. lancifolium* heritage

CHAPTER 5

Lilies for Today's World: The Hybrids

A brief history

Before Jan de Graaf began to make an impact on the gardening scene in the 1950s with his mid-century hybrids bred at Oregon Bulb Farms, virus disease had been a constant enemy of lily growers. Lilies, apart from one or two tough species, had earned the reputation of being short-lived garden plants. One of the aims of his breeding program was to defeat this problem. In the process, he and his fellow hybridizers started producing lilies that revolutionized the status of lilies as garden plants.

Of course, breeders had introduced hybrid lilies with varying degrees of success before this. Cornelis de Graaf, great-grandfather of Jan, started hybridizing lilies in Holland in 1790.

Isabella Preston, who immigrated to Canada from England in 1912 and subsequently was co-organizer of the North American Lily Society, became the first woman hybridist in Canada when she crossed *Lilium regale* with *L. sargentiae* in 1916. 'George C. Creelman', a descendant of this original cross, in turn has contributed its genes to more modern hybrids. She also bred the stenographer hybrids, an important group used extensively by hybridizers at Jan de Graaf's Oregon Bulb Farms.

Edouard Debras, a Frenchman from Orleans, made an important breakthrough when he crossed *Lilium sargentiae* with *L. henryi* in 1925 and so created *L.* x *aurelianense*, which gave birth to the race of lilies known as aurelians.

Opposite: Asiatic hybrids are valuable for their color and form.

Lilium longiflorum flowers in midsummer

In the United States, Dr. David Griffiths, a former professor of botany at the University of Arizona, started working for the United States Department of Agriculture in about 1916. He went on to develop a range of hybrids first known as Griffiths' hybrids but later dubbed Bellingham hybrids after the name

Above: An Aurelian hybrid gained from crossing 'Bright Star' with *Lilium henryi*
Below: A dainty Trumpet hybrid

of the city in Washington State where he lived. He worked with North American species, particularly three native to the West Coast: *Lilium humboldtii* var. *ocellatum*, *L. pardalinum* and *L. parryi*, and the lilies he introduced in 1924 were so successful that they are still available today. For many years these hybrids thrived in special plantings at the Royal Horticultural Society's gardens at Wisley in England. 'Shuksan' and 'Star of Oregon' are two well-known cultivars from this strain. (A strain, sometimes called a "grex," is a group of plants, all derived from crosses of the same parents, which resemble each other but which may exhibit slight variations.)

In spite of these successes, lily hybrids were not held in great regard by the enthusiasts. A measure of just how much regard can be judged by a discussion in 1957 at a meeting of the Royal Horticultural Society Lily Group among several passionate growers. Some questioned whether long-lived hybrids would ever be successful. Some were optimistic. Jan de Graaf's efforts, which were only just becoming apparent, were mentioned as a hopeful indicator. The most definite opinion, however, was expressed by a Dr. Turrill: "Whatever we say at this meeting or anywhere else," he said, "lily experts will go on crossing and back-crossing and making a lovely mess of the plants from a botanical point of view. There is not the slightest reason why they should not do that, but please do not send the results in for naming!"

Contrast this with an encounter in 2002. The International Lily Registrar was visiting New Zealand from Britain and begged Ted Alexander, a New Zealand breeder, to hurry up and name some of his stunning ryirube crosses so they could be registered. (The somewhat clumsy name of ryirube denotes hybrids with *Lilium henryi* and *L. rubellum* genes.) There are now 7,900 named lily hybrids listed on the International Lily Register and probably just as many unregistered.

A feature of the successes achieved in the creation of new hybrids is the almost incredible and

Asiatic 'Honeywind'

ongoing cooperation among breeders in a multitude of countries who come from varied backgrounds. Botanists, research workers, university professors, nurserymen, commercial breeders, a plumber, an architect and inspired hobbyists have all contributed to the pool of knowledge.

In the last 35 years the importance of the lily as a horticultural crop has increased enormously, especially in the Netherlands where most lilies are developed for the cut-flower trade and where the production area has increased from about 250 acres (100 ha) in 1966 to about 12,350 acres (5,000 ha) in 2001.

Nowadays, the number of easy-to-grow lilies is so numerous and varied that it is possible to have them in flower from early summer through until early fall in a wide range of climatic zones.

So diverse are the hordes of hybrids that it can be difficult for the novice lily grower to sort out their various attributes. In 1964 they were classified into eight divisions whose names relate to the species from which the hybrids were bred. (The ninth division is for species.) These were determined by the Lily Committee of the Royal Horticultural Society to assist with the organization of lily shows and were based loosely on the genetic make-up of each group. Since then, increasing numbers of species have been introduced into the genetic brew. Sophisticated modern interventions in the germination process now make inter-divisional crosses and inter-specific crosses successful where once they seemed like the stuff of impossible dreams. The original classification no longer provides a comprehensive representation of the hybrids available and it has been suggested that new divisions need to be introduced based on the look of the plants. While knowing what the divisions are will not make your lilies grow better, it will certainly help you identify lilies you see, understand their attributes and needs and aid in the planning of your garden.

Division I: Asiatic hybrids

This group of hybrids, developed over many years and gradually diversified by the inclusion of a variety of Asian species, has provided gardeners with a huge range of beautiful, hardy plants that have skyrocketed to popularity in recent years.

While many hybridizers in different countries have all played their part in improving the Asiatics, it was at Oregon Bulb Farms where the bulk of the development took place, particularly in producing garden-friendly plants. During the 1930s and 1940s de Graaf sourced early hybrids from as many places as possible. In a massive breeding program that continued for several decades he produced huge quantities of seedlings, including the famous orange 'Enchantment', one of the most influential hybrids ever created. It was introduced into the Netherlands in 1960, eventually becoming the most popular Asiatic lily in the cut-flower trade.

Resistance to virus disease was the driving force in the breeding program at Oregon Bulb Farms and over the years sometimes bitter experience proved that the species *Lilium davidii* imparted virus resistance to its progeny. Its genes were in Isabella Preston's stenographer hybrids and continue to be present in most modern Asiatic hybrid groups.

Once known as mid-century hybrids, the plants bred at Oregon Bulb Farms and their descendants are now known as Asiatic hybrids, the umbrella name used to include a vast array of plants whose genes have been stirred and blended innumerable times. These are the lilies most often admired as cut flowers and most widely grown in gardens worldwide. They are virtually pest-free, they exhibit amazing strength and substance – particularly the newer polyploid hybrids – and vary dramatically in height and color. And they don't need staking.

As if all this isn't enough to recommend them to gardeners, they are incredibly hardy. One grower

Top: An attractive Asiatic hybrid with 'Honeywind' as one parent
Above: Asiatic 'Blue Eyes'

from Manitoba reports that his Asiatics are hardy in zone 3. Another grower located just south of Saskatoon, in zone 2 – one of the colder areas during winters, yet one of the hottest during summers – also reports success with Asiatics.

Of course, nothing is perfect. Asiatics have a distinct lack of fragrance.

Asiatic 'Gran Paradiso'

Their flowers are often large, tend to be close together on the stem and colors are brilliant and wide ranging. The flowers may be upright (Division Ia), outward-facing (Division Ib) or pendent (Division Ic). Florists love them for making vivid, flower-filled bouquets and because of the demands of the cut-flower trade, upward-facing blooms have been an all-important criterion in the creation of modern hybrids. Some come without the freckling often associated with lilies and others come with brushmarks. Originally their colors were limited, ranging through yellows to orange and red. However, so many species are now involved in their family tree that they come in all the warm shades as well as pink and white.

One of the first hybridizers to turn his attention to extending the range of Asiatic colors was Dr.

C. F. Patterson, one-time head of the Department of Horticulture at the University of Saskatchewan, who initiated a lily breeding program in 1935.

His declared aims were to produce hardy lilies in pink and white, and lilies with trumpet form. He succeeded in his first goal, not in his second. By including the Asian species *Lilium davidii* var. *willmottiae*, *L. dauricum* and *L. lancifolium* in his crosses, he introduced winter hardiness into his plants. The genes of *L. cernuum* brought in pink coloration and *L. regale* gave him white. One of his best-known selections, 'Edith Cecilia', named in memory of his daughter and selected in 1944, is an unusual shade of pink and is still considered a valuable plant. It has been used by breeders for the last 50 years as a parent in many modern hybrids. Together with Dr. Bert Porter and Dr. Frank Skinner, an Englishman and a

Legendary Asiatic hybrid 'Enchantment' was first introduced in 1947.

Scot who both lived their adult lives in Canada, he made an important contribution to the development of hardy Asiatic lilies.

The Patterson introductions have now mainly been surpassed. They lost their popularity when the Ia types with upright-facing flowers became sought after. In addition they were susceptible to *botrytis* and *fusarium*, though a few such as 'Golden Princess', 'Jasper', 'Tiger Queen' and 'Red Torch' are still available – they have proven to be survivors.

Two other hybridizers whose work contributed to the strength of the continually improving hybrids were David Stone and Henry Payne. They worked as a partnership seeking to breed Asiatic lilies without spots. Two of their best-known lilies, 'Connecticut Yankee' and 'Nutmegger', were the forerunners of the other famous Connecticut hybrids later developed at Oregon Bulb Farms after Jan de Graaf purchased many of their cultivars.

Fred Fellner is an Alberta farmer who started breeding Asiatic lilies as a hobby in the 1960s. In the process he developed some of the hardiest, most *botrytis*-resistant and sturdy lilies seen in North America. He has developed a wide range of colors – from white to pale pinks through reds to near black and has about 30 registered varieties. Some of his best include 'Red Raven', 'Melissa Jamie', 'Mother Teresa', 'Snow Leopard', 'Red Blaze', 'Parkland Orange' and 'Red Galaxy'. They are strong, hardy and prolific to the extent that gardeners have to divide them every two or three years. Mak-Leek lilies originate in Holland and have mainly outward-facing flowers. They are very hardy, *botrytis*-resistant and cover the color range. Notable are 'Shirley', 'Pink Trophy', 'Conquestador', 'Tristar' and 'Snow Peak'. The Fellner and Mak-Leek lilies are easy to grow (plant properly and forget about them), have great ranges of colors, bicolors and tricolors, offer resistance to both *botrytis* and *fusarium*, and are totally hardy down to zone 2. Blooming season will normally run from early to late summer. Given average weather they will probably bloom for up to two weeks each.

Popular Asian hybrids blooming early/midsummer

'Alaska'	white
'Apeldoorn'	orange
'Connecticut King'	yellow
'Corsica'	pink
'Crete'	deep pink
'Dawn Star'	cream
'Enchantment'	orange
'Gran Paradiso'	red
'London'	yellow
'Naranja'	orange
'Nove Cento'	yellow
'Parkland Orange'	orange
'Pretender'	orange
'Roma'	creamy white
'Vivaldi'	pink

Division II: Martagon hybrids

As the name suggests these are derived from *Lilium martagon* and, initially, *L. hansonii*. Compared to the Asiatics this is a very small group. Because they take longer from seed to flower – between five and seven years – results for hybridizers are slower and commercial interest has been slight.

Quite different in appearance from the Asiatics, the whole plant is dainty, generally of medium to tall height bearing nodding, Turk's cap-shaped flowers that add a sense of Eastern mystery to any garden. Like the species' parents they flower early in the season, enjoy light shade and usually produce lots of flowers. They will also tolerate alkaline soil, thrive in heavy clay and loam but do well in sandy soils, too. Although they love shady places they can

Below: Asiatic 'America'
Bottom: Asiatic 'Tikal'

handle full sun as well and are hardy to zone 3. The color range is wide: white, yellow, orange, tangerine, mahogany, brown, lavender and lilac.

'Marhan', the first well-known hybrid in the group, was produced in 1891 in the Netherlands and is still available. It grows up to 6 ft. (1.8 m) with spotted flowers in a rich, orange-chestnut color.

A group of hybrids from *Lilium martagon* and *L. hansonii*, known as the Backhouse hybrids, was bred at the turn of the 20th century in England by Mrs. R. O. Backhouse, with the best-known cultivar bearing her name.

The Paisley hybrids appeared somewhat later and were a cross between *Lilium martagon* var. *album* and *L. hansonii*. In the second generation, the color range increased. From shades of gold and bronze they broadened to include clearer yellows and oranges as well as white and lilac.

These are normally healthy plants, resistant to virus and very cold hardy. Once planted, they will survive happily in one place for many years. Recently more species have been introduced into the mix and increasingly growers in the cold zones in North America are seeking them out.

Hardy to zone 3.

Division III: Candidum hybrids

This is a small group and includes one of the oldest known hybrids, *Lilium* x *testaceum*, known as the Nankeen lily, a cross made in the early 19th century between *L. candidum* with trumpet-shaped blooms and *L. chalcedonicum*, with bright red Turk's cap-shaped blooms. More recently *L. monadelphum, L.*

Asiatic 'Chianti'

Asiatic 'Grand Cru'

Asiatic 'Last Dance' has pendent blooms.

cernuum, *L. longiflorum* and *L. henryi* have been used in crosses with *L. candidum* and various Asiatic hybrids using embryo rescue techniques. With stems growing to 4 ft. (1.2 m), the flowers are big and fragrant and appear in early summer.

'June Fragrance', bred in 1971 by Judith Freeman in the United States from the variety *Lilium candidum salonikae* with *L. monadelphum*, is a notable hybrid in its own right with creamy white, perfumed flowers in early spring. It has been used in subsequent years as a parent of more hybrids.

Division IV: American hybrids

These are generally tall, stately plants bred from the western or Pacific Coast species of North America. The flowers are mainly Turk's cap-shaped, though less tightly reflexed than some of the species themselves. Like the martagon hybrids, they enjoy light shade, making attractive woodland plants with flowers in late spring or early summer. Best known are the Bellingham hybrids bred from *Lilium humboldtii* var. *ocellatum*, *L. pardalinum* and *L. parryi*.

In England Derek Fox used these to create his Bellmaid hybrids in 1968. Blooms are a rich yellow,

darkening with age and are typically pendent, with reflexed petals. His Bullwood hybrids, introduced the previous year and bringing pink into the color spectrum, resulted in seedlings with peach-toned flowers and others where the typical orange-red of several species becomes a richer red.

'Lake Tahoe' (red and gold), 'Lake Tulare' (crimson-red and gold), 'Oliver Wyatt' (pale amber) and 'Shuksan' (tangerine-gold) are other popular cultivars in this division.

Division V: Longiflorum hybrids

The long elegant trumpets of *Lilium longiflorum*, pure white and fragrant, have ensured its place in the hearts of gardeners and commercial growers for more than 150 years. Over this time, varieties of the species have come and gone while a few have endured because of their commercial value.

Forced to flower for Easter in North America, and flowering outside in gardens in zones 8, 9 and 10 – often in time for Christmas in the Southern Hemisphere – *Lilium longiflorum* has long been valued as a container plant. Much research was carried out in Holland in the early 1980s with the

A Paisley hybrid, member of the Martagon division

aim of producing *Lilium longiflorum* varieties that would satisfy the needs of the commercial market, from both the production point of view and the quality of the material.

This resulted in mass production of bulbs in that country, which continues, and in the last 20 years Israel has also started cultivating bulbs to export to Western Europe for greenhouse growing.

Until recently, however, this species received little attention from hybridizers intent on crossing it with other species. Now it has been crossed with the somewhat similar-looking *Lilium formosanum* to produce vigorous hybrids, primarily of interest to the commercial world.

More importantly it has also been crossed with Asiatic and Trumpet hybrids to produce some beautiful cultivars known as LA hybrids. As these crosses become more complicated the original form of *Lilium longiflorum* becomes less easy to discern.

Division VI: Trumpet hybrids

Talk about Trumpet lilies to gardeners and most will probably think of *Lilium regale* – tall and perfumed with white flowers shaded dark rose-purple on the reverse of its petals, a reliable plant that comes back year after year. But nowadays, as a result of much complex hybridizing, Trumpet lilies come in a range of colors and shapes including sumptuous textured cream blooms with golden throats, dark beauties with a hint of the occult in their purple-black blooms and wonderful golden-copper creations that glow with sunset colors.

These lilies tolerate summer temperatures of 86°F (30°C) and they are hardy to zone 4. Growers in zone 3 report success with some pampering – a good covering of mulch helps regulate the soil temperature, especially where there is no snow cover. With some snow cover for insulation they will survive down to -40°F (-40°C).

Included in this division are two separate streams determined by parentage.

First there are those where the flowers have retained the definite trumpet shape with long bodies and petals flaring out or slightly reflexing at the tips (Division VIa).

They are derived from crossing the species with a pronounced trumpet shape – *Lilium regale*, *L. sargentiae*, *L. leucanthum* var. *centifolium* and *L. sulphureum*, plus *L. henryi* with reflexed petals – together with hybrids created among them in the early decades of the 20th century.

Secondly in this division, there are the Aurelians, demonstrating the influence of *Lilium henryi* genes. These are cultivars with flowers exhibiting three distinctive forms: bowl-shaped (VIb), flat (VIc) or reflexed (VId).

Above: The Copper King strain of Trumpet hybrids glow with warmth.
Above right: A tetraploid Trumpet hybrid, a typically big flower with petals of strong substance
Right: Aurelian, McLaren selection

The first cross between a Trumpet and *Lilium henryi* was the lily created by Monsieur Debras in the 1920s and called *L. x aurelianense*. This cross, plus later hybrids including *L. henryi* in their parentage, were mixed into the existing brew of Trumpet lilies and gave rise to the group name. The inclusion of *L. henryi* in the mix vastly extended the variety of the Trumpets. Many are hardy garden plants in a wide range of conditions.

As with the Asiatics, much of the early hybridizing was done at Oregon Bulb Farms with material gained from many sources. Through careful selection, strong plants carrying a well-arranged pyramid of flowers in shades through white, cream, yellow and pink were produced and originally marketed as centifolium hybrids, later becoming known as Olympic hybrids.

Among the successful selections and crosses were the Black Magic strain with white flowers enhanced by a yellow throat and dark reverses, 'Black Dragon' as the seed parent; the Golden Splendor strain with golden-yellow flowers colored wine on the reverse of the petals, 'Golden Spur' and 'Pioneer' being outstanding cultivars; the Pink Perfection strain with an intense color, deep enough to be called purple, with 'Damson' an outstanding selection and 'Midnight', a strong, disease-resistant plant with rich colored blooms; the Copper King strain, which produces flowers varying from rich orange to more subtle shades of copper and salmon and which initially included an earlier strain called African Queen; the First Love strain with an open form, a spicy fragrance and colors from softest salmon to burnished copper; Sunburst strains with flat or slightly bowl-shaped flowers of which the Golden Sunburst strain has proved to be a resilient garden plant. Also in this group are several upright Trumpet

Above: This richly red Trumpet hybrid is a cross between the Aurelian 'Midnight' and 'Moriarty'. Beside it is a bloom of the Black Dragon strain.
Right: Oriental hybrid, clearly showing its *L. speciosum* parentage

hybrids, the first at Oregon Bulb Farms coming from the American hybridizer LeVern Freimann who worked with *Lilium* x *aurelianense* to produce both Trumpets and Aurelians. It was a golden-yellow hybrid and later an upright pink that came from McLaren, a breeder in New Zealand. A more recent strain, bred at Cebeco Lilies in Oregon, is the Herald Angel strain, a group of strong-growing lilies with big heads of closely arranged flowers looking up to heaven – appropriate, given their name!

Division VII: Oriental hybrids

If you're looking for flamboyant plants to give your garden character after the first flush of summer roses and perennials is over, then look no further than the Oriental hybrids. They are sensational plants, ranging in height from 2–8 ft. (0.6–2.4 m), with wide leaves tapering to a point and producing huge flowers in mid to late summer. Most are perfumed and the newer cultivars are virus-tolerant.

Surprisingly, given their height, even the tall varieties grow well in containers. These lilies are not lime-tolerant and, because they flower from midsummer when the sun is hottest, they prefer some protection from afternoon heat. As the weather cools, the color in late-flowering varieties intensifies.

Derived mainly from the two Japanese species, the large-flowered *Lilium auratum* and *L. speciosum*, the blooms range in color from white through to pink and deep red and include bicolors. Often the red coloring appears to be painted over the white. No orange appears in Orientals and the only yellow appears in the center or rays of the blooms. As with Asiatics, the flowers come in three distinct shapes: bowl-shaped, flat and reflexed.

For many years the two species were difficult to cross, although Francis Parkman succeeded in 1869 producing the hybrid known as *L. x parkmanii*. Two New Zealanders, Leslie Jury and J. S. Yeates, nearly a century later made similar crosses.

Early Oriental hybrids were susceptible to virus disease and this was a continuing difficulty during the history of developing Orientals.

J. S. Yeates, a professor at Massey University in New Zealand, was a pioneer in the breeding of Oriental hybrids and earned an international reputation in breeding both rhododendrons and lilies, his aim with the latter being to produce disease-resistant hybrids. His best known is 'Journey's End', which is vigorous and virus-resistant, alive and well 45 years after its initial introduction. It is still grown extensively and used for forcing in both North America and Europe.

He sent many of his cultivars to Oregon Bulb Farms and they formed the basis of the American

Top right: Oriental 'Muscadet'
Middle right: Oriental 'Rosie Wonder'
Bottom right: Oriental 'Casa Blanca'

company's breeding program in Orientals for many years. His material, along with more from New Zealander Leslie Jury, contributed to the genetic make-up of de Graaf's Imperial Crimson, Imperial Gold and Imperial Silver strains, which produced flowers of great beauty.

Henry Mitchell writes in admiration in *The Essential Earthman* that he had always supposed Jan de Graaf "to be possessed of unearthly powers" and he found the Imperial strains to be irresistible. "They are superlatively worth growing even if transitory."

Another New Zealand cultivar of great importance in the Oriental strains is 'Jillian Wallace', introduced around 1938 and later used by Oregon Bulb Farms to create their Empress selection among others.

J. S. Yeates was also the first to breed dwarf Orientals and from some of his selected clones and seed, Oregon Bulb Farms developed their Little Rascals strain, which makes for excellent small container plants.

The Orientals have been hugely successful in Australia and New Zealand and in the last 15 years hybridization has taken off in spectacular fashion in both the United States and in Holland, particularly in the cut-flower industry.

This was sparked by the introduction of the beautiful crimson-red 'Star Gazer', the first upright-facing Oriental hybrid, bred by American Leslie Woodriff. Woodriff was a pioneer in the breeding of these hybrids, being one of the first breeders to include the species *Lilium japonicum* and *L. rubellum* as parents to widen the gene pool of Orientals.

Subsequently two more species were introduced into the group: *Lilium alexandrae* and *L. nobilissimum*, thereby further extending the possible outcome of crosses.

Woodriff's 'Black Beauty', found in 1957 as a chance seedling in a field of lilies and later discovered to be a cross between *Lilium henryi* with *L. speciosum* var. *rubrum*, has entered into the North American Lily Society's Hall of Fame, and is still used in its tetraploid form as an important breeding parent.

Orientals in cold climates

Although difficult to grow successfully where summers are warm and humid, Orientals are recognized as being hardy to zone 3 – in Northern Minnesota (zone 3), one gardener who gets lots of snow cover in winter reports that specifically 'Stargazer', 'Star Fighter', 'Casa Blanca' and 'Versailles' have done well for her. Success seems to vary from grower to grower, but gardeners are a persistent lot. We don't give in easily.

Canadian growers in the prairie provinces have devised ways and means of bringing their lilies through the winter. Some grow them in containers in greenhouses or grow them in containers that they remove to a cold room for overwintering. Most recommend spring planting of Orientals to give them a whole season to get firmly established before the cold weather. Planting them deeply – at least 8 in. (20 cm) to the base of the bulb – is also important. All recommend mulching to try to prevent the repeated freeze/thaw cycle, which is damaging.

One gardener in zone 2 digs the bulbs up in fall and replants them deeply along the edge of the basement wall. Another grower, in zone 3, believes

LA hybrid 'Royal Victory'

Asiatic 'Tiger Babies' is valuable for its unusual coloring.

the problem lies with a short season that does not give the lilies sufficient time for the bulb to replenish itself after flowering and before frosts arrive. So, he plants his bulbs in spring in 2-gal. (9-l) plastic containers. When the stem emerges, the plant is watered daily with a soluble fertilizer added. Plants flower from mid to late summer, and after flowering the heads are cut off and the containers are moved to a cooler location. Feeding stops – though not watering – and the plants are left to mature.

Once the stems have been removed after one or two frosts – usually early fall – the containers are buried in the ground with soil heaped over them and above ground level for 3–4 in. (7.5–10 cm) in the expectation of 2–3 ft. (60–100 cm) of snow. Come March or April, the containers are dug up and placed inside in a basement to thaw.

When growth starts again the containers are moved to an area behind glass and when temperatures reach about 46°F (8°C), they go outside during daylight hours. About the beginning of May the temperatures are warm enough for the lilies to be left outside day and night.

Some popular and enduring Oriental hybrids

'Acapulco'	'Allegra'
'Black Beauty'	'Casa Blanca'
'Cascade'	'Crimson Beauty'
'Journey's End'	'Laura Lee'
'Le Rêve'	'Marco Polo'
'Muscadet'	'Olympic Star'
'Pink Beauty'	'Red Jewel'
'Shooting Star'	'Star Gazer'
'Tom Pouce'	'Woodriff's Memory'

New age lilies

As long ago as the 1960s, hybridizers realized that if they could increase the chromosome count in lilies, among other plants, they would increase the range within which crosses could be made. At the same time they would increase the strength of plants, the substance of their petals and the intensity of flower color. This was achieved by treating a plant with the normal number of chromosomes – usually a diploid with 24 chromosomes – with the chemical colchicine, obtained from *Colchicum autumnale*,

Orienpet 'Northern Carillon'

and transforming it into a tetraploid with 48 chromosomes.

Another technique called embryo culture (EC) can be used when distantly related lilies produce a few viable embryos in a seedpod, but no endosperm to nurture the seed. The technique involves extracting the healthy embryo and removing it to a chemical nutrient solution.

Arthur Evans, director of the North American Lily Society and a keen amateur breeder, was thinking of this process when he said, "Hybrids from different horticultural divisions of the genus *Lilium* are very hesitant to cross with each other. Species can be even more picky about partners. And yet, with persistence and special techniques, sometimes we can coax a miracle out of unlikely and unwilling pairs."

The miracles are new hybrids created by crossing breeding boundaries once thought impenetrable.

One of the pioneers among the miracle workers is Judith Freeman. In the early 1970s she worked at Oregon Bulb Farms concentrating on the technique of EC, thus inducing crosses between species not previously included in their hybrid program and extending the range of hybrids across Asiatics, Orientals and Orienpets. Among many others 'Tiger

Babies' was a notable success. Derived on one side of its family from 'Pink Tiger', a hybrid of *Lilium lancifolium* with *L. regale*, it is still available and is a highly desirable plant with a rather insouciant air to it. Think of a pastel peach version of a tiger lily.

LeVern Freimann succeeded in producing some spectacular tetraploid Asiatics including a tetraploid form of the already famous 'Black Beauty', which was crucial in the subsequent development of the Orienpets.

Also in the United States, Edward McRae has worked extensively with polyploid hybrids, seeking always to produce plants that are disease-resistant and garden friendly.

Peter Schenk, a well-known hybridizer in the Netherlands, learned much of his trade at Oregon Bulb Farms and has gone on to produce some spectacular tetraploid Asiatic hybrids as well as smaller varieties of Asiatics for container culture. Wilbert Ronald and Lynn Collicut in Canada are well-known for their hardy Orienpets.

Dr. Chris North, working in Edinburgh in the 1970s, used the EC technique with the graceful *Lilium lankongense*, *L. davidii* and various Asiatic hybrids to breed a series of quite different plants from those the North American breeders have worked on.

His hybrids were distinguished by graceful pyramids of hanging flowers with reflexed petals.

Division VIII – All other hybrids

LA hybrids

This category of hybrid lily was introduced to the market in 1992, with the initials that compose the name coming from the parent plants: Longiflorum lilies and various Asiatic hybrids. The result of this cross is a race of lilies that are hardy and long-lived as a cut flower. Blooms are mainly outward-facing; they tend to be large and are often fragrant. This is not all. They are disease-resistant and tolerant of virus infection. And, an important attribute for gardeners, they multiply quickly. So it's no wonder that this lily, initially bred for the cut-flower trade, is becoming a popular garden plant.

LAs are common in gardens in Canada where temperatures can plunge to -35°F (-37°C) and lower in winter (zone 3). Many varieties are available; some have inflorescences that are very crowded. Because they are fast multipliers they need to be replanted every three to four years.

Orienpet hybrids

This new group of hybrids between Orientals and Trumpets or Aurelians (and all the species that have contributed their genes to the common pool) combines the beauty and fragrance of the former with the adaptability and colors of the latter. In climates where summers are too warm for Orientals to thrive, the Orienpets take over, coming into bloom three to four weeks after the Asiatics. They are high performers in gardens from coast to coast across the United States; in Canada, growers in the cold prairie provinces are enthusiastic about their success, though they recommend mulching for winter protection.

Many of the flowers have deeply reflexed petals with Oriental lily colors while others have the color and character of the regale lilies but with outward, open petals. Most are large plants, often 6.5–8 ft. (2–2.5 m) tall with 20–60 blooms that are sensational for several weeks in the summer. So far the Orienpets as a group are not very fertile, though many crosses will form embryos without endosperm and this hybrid group is benefiting greatly from the use of embryo culture.

Some of the best of these hardy, beautiful lilies, thriving in zones 3–9, are 'Scheherazade', 'Northern Carillon', 'Silk Road', 'Starburst Sensation', 'Northern Sensation' and 'Leslie Woodriff'. From Canada comes 'Regal Star' bred by Dick Bazett, and 'Easter Morn' and 'Northern Star' from the partnership of Wilbert Ronald and Lynn Collicutt.

Canadian Belles series

This is a new series of lilies combining the fragrance and other attributes of the Aurelian Trumpets with hardy Asiatics. Only a small group, they were bred in Canada for prairie conditions, come in a range of colors, are particularly resistant to *botrytis* and *fusarium* and are hardy, with mulching, in zone 2. Blooms are big and they come into flower just after the Asiatics. The names are easy to recognize and give an indication of their color. Among them are 'Blushing Belles', 'Creamy Belles', 'Firey Belles' and 'Purple Belles'.

LA hybrid 'Royal Sunset'

CHAPTER 6

Planting Ideas

Setting the stage

Of all flowers after the rose, it is the lily that has attracted the most attention in literature and in art. Madonna lilies have graced gardens for centuries but it is in florists' shops today that we most often see lilies taking center stage. We drool over the classic white blooms of *Lilium longiflorum*; we smile at the blooms of Asiatics arranged in appealing, bright bouquets. But lilies seen in gardens often lack

the "wow" factor. The flowers are gorgeous, but, too often it seems, they have no sense of cohesion with their neighbors.

Lilies are stars; few of them fit into the chorus. But equally, star quality is diminished if the supporting cast is inadequate. Lilies need a stage set where their form can be admired.

Vita Sackville-West understood this. She wrote about liking to see lilies in her garden "…piercing up

Roses and lilies satisfy the heart of any gardener who loves perfume and color.

Trumpet hybrids look dramatic with evergreens as a background. 'Bright Star' is at the rear to the left.

between low, grey-foliaged plants such as artemisia, southernwood and santolina, and rising above some clouds of gypsophila." She liked the contrasting shapes of the domed bushes and the belfry-like tower of the lily, which she thought created an architectural harmony.

You may have fallen in love with a particular lily and in this case you will most likely seek it out at all costs and make space for it in your garden. But if it is lilies in general that interest you, then think a little about the character of your garden before deciding on the actual plant.

Some lilies are tall and elegantly structured; some are almost ethereal in their beauty; yet others are strong characters with big, bold clumping blooms. The dwarf *Lilium nanum*, growing about 12 in. (30 cm) high is suitable for the rock garden. So are some of the smaller varieties of *L. longiflorum*. The 8-ft.

(2.5-m) giants like *L. henryi* just have to go at the back of a border or be tucked in beside substantial shrubs. Remember, it's not only their color that will impact on your design, but also their form, as Sackville-West points out.

Think also about the flowers and the way they show themselves. If you have fallen in love with an Asiatic with big upward-facing blooms you want to be able to look into them and enjoy their beauty. No point if you have to climb a stepladder to do it! Alternatively, if it is a plant that hangs its flowers shyly, a lot of its impact will be lost if you look down on its blooms.

Many are tall narrow plants, rushing to reach the sky in spring. The stems, furred with leaves, initially fit into the general scheme of growth. But summer arrives, suddenly they're beanstalk height, buds are forming and they tower over the other perennials.

We've all seen them: lilies in the wrong place and looking awkward. The single Asiatic hybrid creating a blob of color that absolutely refuses to cohabit comfortably with less emphatic flowers – as out of place as an exclamation mark in the middle of a sentence.

Or a stiff row of candidums set up on sentinel duty along a boundary fence. Or regales appearing in random ones and twos, isolated and straggly.

Don't do it. Dig them up and replant them – but wait till fall. Put them in family groups. People like others of the same ilk around them; so, too, with plants. And once you have the lilies comfortable with each other, provide them with one or two tall companions – delphiniums, verbascums or penstemons, for example.

Tall varieties need to be planted where they won't overwhelm shorter plants – usually at the back of a border with a wall or a hedge for background, though hedge plants are thirsty creatures that suck up moisture and you need to make sure the lilies are not deprived. Try leaving at least 2 ft. (60 cm) between hedge and border plants. It won't be visible when the lilies and other perennials grow up; it gives access to the hedge when it needs trimming; it offers space for mulching and the border plants will appreciate the gap between their roots and the roots of the hedge.

Companions with class

By planting lilies in a border with carefully selected perennials, you can enjoy a prolonged season of color as well as a supply of cut flowers. If possible, include Asiatics, regales and Orientals – providing them with the right soil, of course – and you will have lilies in bloom from the beginning of summer into early fall so long as you are not affected by untimely frosts.

Peonies produce their blooms in early summer; plant Orientals among them to provide color and

Planted by a florist with unerring instincts

fragrance later. Add some hydrangea bushes with flower colors to coordinate with the lilies. Complete the picture, if it's a big bed, with lower-growing perennials or shrubs in front of them that gradually decrease in height so there is not a vast gap between the lily blooms and the soil.

Lady's mantle (*Alchemilla mollis*) and *Eupatorium rugosum* ('Chocolate') are wonderful to plant at the lilies' feet for sites in full sun, and are hardy to zone 4. Shrubs such as *Caryopteris*, with small blue flowers in late summer, and *Cornus stolonifera* 'Silver and Gold' also fit the bill in full sun.

And remember that lilies, like peonies, put up tender shoots in spring, which are easily damaged if stepped on. Lilies don't produce another shoot until the following season. So it's "goodbye flowers" if this happens. To avoid this mishap, mark where you plant your lily bulbs in fall.

Rhododendrons make good companions. They require the acidic soil conditions that many lilies favor. Their flowering season is well over before that of the lilies so their bold blooms won't clash or compete, and their defined foliage shape provides a harmonious background for bright lily flowers. Camellias also.

Short lilies combine well with small or medium shrubs, which provide shade for the lily roots and some protection from wind. Their foliage can emphasize the form and color of the flowers if the shrubs are chosen to create a specific effect. Silver foliage, for example, such as that of *Teucrium fruticans*, combined with white lilies produces a cool look. A purple barberry, *Berberis thunbergii* 'Atropurpurea' perhaps, or *B. thunbergii* 'Rose Glow', with uniformly small crimson-purple leaves, planted with orange or red lilies gives the opposite effect.

Hebes, a tremendously varied group of plants, give a choice of shrubs with compact growth. Many of them thrive on frequent clipping – *Hebe topiaria* is a good example – and shaped into rounded hummocks or squared-off pillars, they complement the silhouette of lilies. Then imagine the drama of

Top: For those who like brilliant color
Above: *Lilium regale* combines with bright Asiatic lilies in a woodland planting.

a purple-leafed cotinus with the fiery orange Asiatic hybrid 'Gran Paradiso' in front of it.

As with hedges it is important that the shrubs do not gobble up all the water. And remember to plant the lilies in groups.

'Nova Cento' is another bold, in-your-face Asiatic, bright yellow in color. Combine it with deep purple flowers to create a sizzling arrangement – there are several salvias that would give

'Tiger Babies', a lily for the non-traditional gardener

the required color. Try astilbes, with their feathery flowers and fern-like foliage, intermingled with the bolder form of lilies – pale ones maybe – for another totally different look.

Or go for green and white: hostas with creamy white variegations in the leaves, white flowering hydrangeas behind them and low-growing *Lilium longiflorum* varieties mingling with the hostas – *L. longifolium* 'Dutch Glory' produces generous numbers of large, smooth trumpets; a low clipped boxwood hedge with white lilies looking out over it bordering a courtyard; white Oriental 'Casa Blanca', with its head up among the foliage of the white banksia rose, which flowers in spring and the white Flowercarpet Rose, which flowers in summer, at its knees.

Alternatively, choose as neighbors plants that flower at the same season but that produce blooms with a contrasting shape. Asiatic lilies and English roses, for example, make compatible bedmates. They both like sun and the roses won't be overpowered by the lilies; their foliage can offer a support system; the big rose flowers have sufficient substance to provide balance beside a head of lily bloom and it's easy to find colors that are complementary.

The tall dainty martagons, with delicately balanced blooms, impart a sense of otherworldliness and this is the feeling to exploit in a planting of these exotic-looking members of the family. They prosper in light shade so are ideal for creating evocative plantings in light woodland settings. But they are busy plants. Often bearing 20 or more small flowers, their wonderful form can be lost if they are planted too closely.

Hostas with their large leaves provide an ideal foil for the complicated blooms of martagons.

Lilium martagon var. *album* is one to use in a dark corner under a tree or among ferns, and it looks great among mauve-blue campanulas – again the flower shape contrasts and doesn't compete with the martagon – while the lilac-pink species can be used to create a cottage-garden effect, mingling with tall pink *Centranthus ruber*, foxgloves and perhaps an old-world dianthus at its feet.

If you really adore lilies and have the space, then grow great collections of them in your front garden where they will raise their heads over the fence to nod at passers-by and draw great gasps of admiration. Plant Asiatics to flower in early summer, regales for mid-season, Orientals and LA hybrids to continue the show and fit in a few species such as *Lilium pardalinum* to add spice and a touch of the exotic. If your garden is enclosed then not only will it look wonderful but the air will be redolent with perfume.

Come fall in temperate climates you may need to roll in a truckload of containerized shrubs to fill the space, but why not go for broke when the season is right?

Lilies in containers

Growing lilies in containers is an excellent way to exploit their landscaping possibilities. Even tall, heavy hybrids like the Oriental 'Casa Blanca' enjoy being confined to limited living quarters. A patio

Tall Oriental 'Activa' is equally at home in a pot (right) as is the low growing variety of *Lilium longiflorum* (above).

is the ideal place to show them off at the height of the season, or a container of flowering lilies can be moved into a perennial bed at a moment's notice to provide a shot of drama.

Think about the size of the container relative to the size of the plant. Dwarf lilies will look fine in short containers (and will have enough space to grow) but for all other varieties choose a tall rather than a squat container. The lilies will have more space, more access to nutrients and will be less likely to topple over in windy conditions.

Grow them in part or full sun. Strong-colored lilies develop stronger colors in good light; delicate pastels keep their colors longer if protected from strong afternoon sun. As Orientals bloom in mid to late summer when days are often very hot, they prefer shade in the afternoon. Once flowering is over, the exhausted lilies can be retired to a secluded corner to gather their forces for another summer.

For how to grow lilies in containers see Chapter 3 on cultivation.

Dwarf lilies

There's a limited range of dwarf lilies ideal for the front of the border and for containers. These are the ones to group together in color-coordinated clusters on patios or beside a pool. For a splash of color beside the barbecue, arrange to have a series of potted lilies coming into flower in succession and move them into the spotlight when they come into their full glory. Better still, you can have color and perfume if you choose to grow dwarf Oriental lilies.

A group of cultivars developed at Oregon Bulb Farms or bred by Edward McRae, all with 'Pixie' in their name, are reliable plants in a good range of colors, all strong growers and disease resistant.

Short varieties of *Lilium longiflorum* grow well in containers, too, or add an accent for a short period of time among low perennials such as petunias or scabiosa in warm areas (zones 8–10).

For a list of good dwarf varieties see Chapter 3, page 28.

CHAPTER 7

Lilies for Free: Propagation

Better by far than gambling on horses is how one enthusiast describes propagating his own lilies. Dealing with magic is how others see it; to the commercial lily breeder it's a blend of experience, knowledge and science. However you look at it, propagating your own plants is an intriguing occupation and lilies more than most other plants offer several easy options.

New plants can be grown by division of the bulb, from scales, from bulblets that form underground on the stem between the bulb and the soil surface, from bulbils that form in the leaf axils on some species and from viable seed. If you move into the laboratory, then tissue culture is another way of creating new plants – but I'll leave that method to the scientists.

Seed beginnings

Propagating lilies from seed has one distinct advantage over all the other methods available to amateurs: virus disease is not passed on via seeds. Even if both pod parent and pollen parent are infected, the children will start life free of contamination.

Each plant produced by seed is a unique individual and has its own set of genes, as does a person. However, species breed true to type and will usually look the same as their parents, although in some species slight variations do occur.

Plants raised by vegetative means (cuttings, root divisions, or in the case of lilies, bulb scales,

Opposite: *Lilium nepalense* has a rare beauty.
Right: Stem bulbils are clearly visible on this plant.

Asiatic 'Sorrento'

bulbils or bulblets) are clones with a DNA identical to that of their parent, and this is how hybrids are kept true; seeds from hybrids will give a variety of seedling plants. For the naturally inquisitive raising these seedlings can be a source of great interest and it's just possible that you may stumble across a plant of enduring beauty.

Seedpods take several weeks to mature after the flowers have died. Each pod is divided into three compartments, separated by a thin membrane, and the seeds are tidily stacked in each one. The pod is ripe when it dries and splits open at the top and the seed can be shaken out. With some late-flowering varieties it may be necessary to cut off the pod and ripen it in a dry, airy place indoors. Once the wet weather arrives, the pods tend to become sodden, fungus spores can attack and the seed is destroyed.

Most lilies produce prolifically and the pods are usually packed with seeds but there will also be a certain amount of chaff – seeds that have not been fertilized. To check whether individual disk-shaped seeds are viable, hold them up to the light with a pair of tweezers or shake the seeds onto a sheet of thin paper over a light source. If no embryo outline is visible within a capsule, throw it away.

Once you have saved the seeds, they need to be kept dry and stored, preferably in the refrigerator, until sowing in late winter or early spring. The longer they are kept after this time, the less fertile they become. One grower, however, reports success with old seeds after soaking them for a week. Another gardener places hers in a bag made of permeable fabric and hangs them in the back of the toilet for a week!

Seeds are best sown indoors, into trays of seed-starting medium and lightly covered by a layer of fine vermiculite, sand or grit up to 0.25 in. (6 mm) deep. This helps prevent damping off, a fungus disease that attacks small seedlings. Well-spaced seedlings, which allow for good air circulation, are also less likely to succumb to damping off. Spray lightly with water and place the tray in a warm spot. The soil mix must remain moist to ensure germination.

When the young seedlings have emerged and start growing in their trays, they resemble blades of grass. Before they become root-bound they need to be separated out and planted in small containers. Grow the plants in a cool outdoor shed or sink the containers in the ground under a tree or in some other shady place. Make sure they are kept moist but not soggy.

The species *Lilium formosanum*, in favorable conditions, will flower in its first season. Expect Asiatic, Trumpet and Oriental hybrids to flower in their second season. Martagons may take seven years from seed to flower.

Sowing the seeds is not difficult. Knowing when to expect the seedlings to appear is more complicated. Lily seeds germinate in two ways, depending on the variety: they may germinate immediately or after a delay.

Asiatic 'Red Beauty'

Epigeal germination

Once planted, the seed may concentrate first on sending up a seed leaf (cotyledon) then get to work on forming a bulb and pushing up its first true leaf. Other leaves follow during the growing season. This is called epigeal or above-ground germination, and most epigeal seeds germinate immediately. The cotyledon should appear within a few weeks after sowing, so long as the mix has been kept damp. Asiatic, Aurelian and Trumpet hybrids produce epigeal-type seeds.

Hypogeal germination

Alternatively, the seed may turn its first efforts to forming a slender bulb underground and developing a root system before sending up its first true leaf. This is called hypogeal or below ground germination, and most hypogeal germination is delayed. That first leaf may not appear for several months. Oriental lilies are hypogeal germinators.

Some hypogeal-type seeds may need a second year cycle to germinate. For this reason many gardeners sow their seeds in a container that is large enough and deep enough to leave the seeds undisturbed for two years. Those that do germinate have

the space to grow and those that take longer are not wasted by being tipped out.

Hypogeal germination requires first a warm period to initiate the growing of the small bulb. It

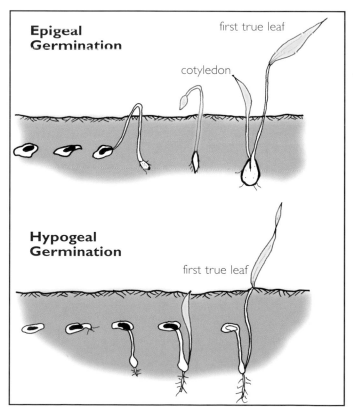

then requires several weeks of cool temperatures, preferably almost at freezing point, to trigger the growth of the leaves.

Seeds of this type, planted in late summer, can take advantage of the end of the warm weather and the natural follow-on of winter, and a season in their development can effectively be short-circuited. But planted in early spring one year, these seeds may not appear above ground until the following spring.

It is possible to imitate the natural cycle by sowing slow-germinating seeds at the beginning of winter in dampened sphagnum moss, sealed in a plastic bag and stowed in a warm, dark place, such as a furnace room, for about three months. The bags should then be placed in the refrigerator for three weeks, and when potted at the end of this time the little bulbs will make top growth immediately.

See Chapter 4 for germination details of the individual species.

Bulb division

If you lift bulbs at the end of summer you will find that the original bulb has produced several new little bulbs, which, in most cases, can easily be broken away. If the bulb is rhizomatous in form you will probably need a knife to cut through its matted base. Detach a section that has attached to it at least one growing point with a new little cluster of pale scales, which will eventually develop into an adult-sized bulb. These new bulbs need to be replanted immediately before they have a chance to dry out.

Where bulbs are left in place for several seasons, the juvenile bulbs will detach from the parent and start producing flowers.

Most lilies are best left in peace to clump for several years before being divided. Only if they start to lose vigor and look unhealthy should they be disturbed earlier.

Bulb scales

It is easy to remove the outside scales from large bulbs and use these as beginning points for new plants.

Asiatic 'London'

This is a practical way to increase your lily plants fast. Once the flowers and stems have died down in fall you can dig down in the soil and remove several scales from each bulb without actually digging it up. Of course, the bulb should be a healthy one – any disease present in it will be passed on through the scales. Dusting the scales with a fungicide is sensible protection in any case.

The following method is a practical way to produce lots of small bulbs in one operation. Choose a deep container and put in a layer of drainage material, then a layer of sphagnum moss covered with a layer approximately 1.5 in. (4 cm) deep of mixed coarse sand, compost and peat or leaf mold. Now place as many scales as will fit, spacing them 1 in. (2.5 cm) apart, and pointing upward. Cover this layer with another 1.5 in. (4 cm) of soil mixture and another set of scales.

Continue in this fashion until the container is full and cover it with sphagnum moss. The soil needs to be kept moist but not wet. Place the container in semi-shade. Several weeks later you should have a quantity of tiny bulbs ready to plant out in containers. Scales from Asiatic hybrids take six to eight weeks, Trumpets eight to 10 weeks and Orientals 12 to 14 weeks.

Stem bulblets

These are mini-bulbs that grow on the underground part of the stem, between the parent bulb and the surface of the soil. They are easy to prise off the stem once it has died back in fall. Each is ready to grow, complete with scales and tiny roots. Pot them in humus-rich potting mix and transfer them carefully to the garden in spring, taking care not to damage their roots.

The production of these stem bulblets can be encouraged by pampering the main plant through the growing season with a rich mulch. Asiatic hybrids tend to be prolific producers of stem bulblets, as are *Lilium lancifolium*, *L. henryi* and *L. regale* and their hybrids.

Species with stoloniferous stems such as *Lilium duchartrei* and *L. nepalense* form a few bulbs as they wander along underground. One gardener reports that her original plant of *L. nepalense* had long since disappeared but existing plants were blooming yards away from where the initial bulb was planted a number of years ago. No doubt the old bulbs had disappeared and the newer bulbs continued producing flowering stems as they moved through her garden.

Stem bulbils

A few species and their hybrids produce tiny bulbils above ground in the axils where the leaf joins the stem. *Lilium lancifolium* is well-known for this behavior. As the season progresses they are very visible as small, round blackish marbles sitting in the leaf joints.

In their own time they will drop to the ground, pull themselves into the soil and start producing roots. But they also can be harvested, potted and they will develop into worthwhile bulbs. The best time to do this is a few weeks after flowering.

The formation of bulbils can be encouraged by cutting off the flower buds (if you can bear to sacrifice the flowers) or by burying the stem. Once the plant has flowered, pull out the stalk, lay it on its side in a shallow trench and cover it with a mixture of peat and sand, leaving a few inches of the tip exposed. After a couple of months you should have plenty of bulbs to grow on. Once again, choose only plants that are disease-free to propagate in this fashion. Of course, the bulbils will be true to type.

Plants propagated from scales, bulbils and bulblets will bloom two or three years after planting.

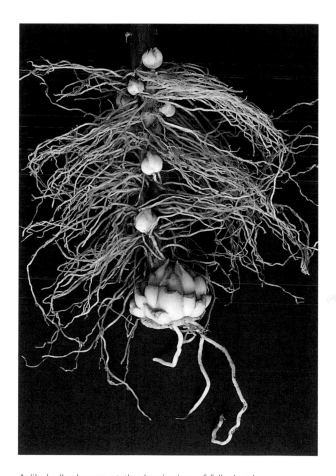

A lily bulb dug up at the beginning of fall, clearly showing the contractile roots at the base of the bulb, the stem roots and several bulblets that have formed on the stem

CHAPTER 8

Lilies on Display

Big, bold, beautiful and long-lasting. It is no wonder lilies have become one of the most admired cut flowers in today's world. Italians idolize them and the French flaunt them; Americans adore them, and lilies are number five after roses, chrysanthemums, carnations and tulips on the list of top 10 flowers sold at the famous cut-flower auctions in Holland.

LAs, Orientals and Asiatics are the lilies most commonly seen on sale but Easter lily (*Lilium longiflorum*) hybrids are increasing in popularity. Interestingly, while most gardeners cherish perfumed plants and therefore like Oriental lilies, market research in the Netherlands has shown that their perfume is often too strong indoors and in recent years the Dutch have been developing Orientals with little or no perfume.

The hybridizing of lilies is driven more than most other popular garden flowers by the needs of the cut-flower market. Bell-shaped flowers or those with the Turk's cap shape do not pack well for transporting, so any species or their hybrids with upward-facing flowers have been rigorously selected and used as parents for a big percentage of modern cultivars. It seems also that unspotted flowers are more popular than those with freckles.

With more than 7,900 named cultivars listed on the International Lily Register and probably about the same number not registered, there is a lily for every occasion. They are available every day of the year in florists' shops, supermarkets and corner stores. We use them to celebrate at weddings and to mourn at funerals; they adorn hospital rooms,

'Tiara', an Oriental popular with brides because it carries no pollen

churches, luxurious functions and simple private homes. Few people in the Western world would not recognize a lily flower.

Tougher than you think

Without a doubt, flowers need to be handled with care when they are picked for display to make sure they look their best indoors. But the flowers themselves are tougher than you may think. The risk is that buds or flowers will snap off.

When buying lilies, choose a stem where the lowest bud has just opened. This way you will have a continuation of flowers opening and the lower blooms can be removed as they fade. If you are picking lilies from your garden, try to pick them in the cool of the morning. Make sure you leave at least two-thirds of the stem on the plant – it is needed to nourish the bulb for the following season.

Recut the lily stems as soon as you bring them indoors and immediately plunge them into a container of water at room temperature; leave them there for several hours to give them the opportunity for a long leisurely drink.

Before arranging them, add a sprinkling of fresh flower preservative, a dash of sugar, an aspirin or one tablespoon of household bleach to the water – these will all help to lengthen the flowers' vase life.

Take off the lower leaves so no foliage remains underwater. Soggy leaves look ugly – not to mention their odor – and they encourage the growth of bacteria. The water should be changed frequently – daily if the lilies are in a transparent container – and don't forget to replace the preservative at the same time.

Place the arranged lilies away from direct sunlight, hot and cold drafts and bowls of fruit. Ripening fruit emits ethylene gas, which shortens the life of flowers, particularly lilies.

Because lilies are spectacular in their own right it is easy to make an attractive, simple arrangement with only one stem, complemented by foliage that does not distract from the star performer.

What about the pollen?

The pollen on the anthers of lilies is seen as a real problem by some. Nurses in white uniforms hate it! But it does add to the appearance of the flowers so it seems a shame to cut it off.

However, if you do get some on your clothes, let it dry then carefully brush it away with a dry soft brush or facial tissue. Sticky tape works well, too, dabbed lightly and repeatedly over the stain. Should some traces of pollen still remain, place the fabric in

Oriental lilies for a modern décor

the sun for a few hours. The stain will disappear.

If you try to brush the pollen away with your fingers the oils from your skin will set the color. Attacking it with water or a damp cloth is equally unsuccessful, as the stain will spread.

'Tiara', one of the newer Oriental lilies, has been bred specifically to have no pollen on its anthers. Brides love it.

CHAPTER 9

Pests and Diseases

Lilies have enjoyed a much more favorable press since the development of hybrids that are tolerant of the dreaded virus infections. Not all lily enemies have been annihilated, however. A gardener in Oregon, writing in the 60th anniversary lily journal of the Royal Horticultural Society, listed the pests that attack lilies in the following order: dogs, mice, moles, deer, rabbits, pheasants and grandchildren. Rather a varied list – too bad if you have to deal with every one of these creatures.

If voles or other animal pests are munching on your cherished bulbs, spraying them with a product such as Ropel may protect them. To ward off underground marauders try placing Vole Block or a small quantity of sharp rock chips around the bulbs to help create a physical barrier, or make short trenches when planting and enclose the bulbs in tubes of wire mesh. The holes in the mesh need to be large enough to allow the shoots to grow through, but small enough to keep the voles out.

A product called Deer Off, which claims to be biodegradable and made from organic components, has had some success in repelling deer. It comes in spray form and must be applied when the first leaves come through the ground and on a continuing basis until the plants bloom.

As for grandchildren – well, transforming them into gardeners is probably a long-lasting solution!

As with all plants, healthy lilies are more resistant to disease attack than neglected and poorly

Asiatic 'Navona'

Lilium martagon 'Album' is tough and beautiful.

grown plants. Keeping them well-fed, well-drained and sufficiently watered is the first step. Providing soil that is compatible with the individual plant's needs – be it species or cultivar – is another important aspect of good health.

Lilies, particularly the hybrids, are greedy plants and if the soil they grow in becomes depleted they will weaken. Some growers recommend moving the bulbs to a new area when they are dug up and divided but this is often not possible for home gardeners. Adding plenty of compost, stirring up the soil before the bulbs are replanted and adding well-rotted horse or cow manure is a good substitute.

A pre-winter tidy up around the lilies helps to get rid of diseases and bugs lurking in decaying leaves where they lie in wait over winter, preparing to inflict more damage the following spring. It is best to burn the leaves if possible. Putting them in the compost bin will spread any fungus disease they may harbor.

If you decide intervention is necessary to control aphids or lily beetle, be aware that chemical insecticides act in two different ways. Systemic insecticides, usually applied by spraying leaves and stems, are absorbed by the plant and carried by the sap to all its living parts. Any insects sucking the sap will be killed. Systemic insecticides protect the plant for a specified length of time. Contact insecticides are exactly that. They kill any insect they hit and are applied as sprays, dusts or smokes. Many of these contain malathion. Less potentially damaging organic insecticides, containing pyrethrum, are available.

Care must be taken at all times when dealing with chemical pesticides or fungicides. Used carelessly they can be dangerous to humans and animals; residues can remain in the soil for a long time with the risk of entering into the food chain. It is important to follow the manufacturer's instructions, to always label any containers used to dispense pesticides and to keep them out of reach of children, preferably locked away when not in use. Protective clothing should be worn and care taken not to inhale any fumes.

After use, be sure to remove all the residue from the container. What you remember using as a dispenser for insecticide may in fact have been used to hold weed killer. Next time you use the container, you do not want to kill the whole plant instead of only the insects on it!

Sprays are easily carried by wind so choose a day with calm weather and do any necessary spraying in the evening when bees are less active. Remember that insecticides can't think; they are unable to distinguish between good bugs, such as ladybugs, and bad bugs, such as greenfly, which the ladybugs eat. "How damaging are those insects?" we need to ask ourselves before we reach for the killer sprays.

Pests

Aphids, including greenfly

The appearance of aphids on your lily flowers is bad news! All gardeners are familiar with greenfly, those tiny insects that swarm onto plants at the height of the growing season and greedily suck the sap, leaving a sticky honeydew in their wake. They multiply at an alarming rate and like other aphids they look unsightly, their sap-sucking habits debilitate plants and, most seriously, they often transmit virus from diseased plants to healthy ones. As well as carrying virus, aphids also weaken the plants, causing leaves to twist and buds to be malformed.

If you grow only a few plants (and have amazing persistence) it may be possible to control these annoying insects by physically squashing them on a continuing basis or by dousing them liberally with a fast jet of water from the hose.

Systemic pesticides are effective either by spraying, which needs to be repeated at regular intervals, over summer or by watering it into the soil.

Aphids tend to proliferate in greenhouses and need to be controlled.

Some gardeners report success in controlling aphids with an organic tea made from rhubarb leaves.

Organic anti-aphid spray
1 lb. (0.5 kg) rhubarb leaves
2.5 pt. (1.5 l) of water
Simmer the leaves in the water for 30 mins. Strain the mixture and store in a glass jar – this is now the rhubarb extract. When ready to use, add 1 fl. Oz. (28 ml) of dishwashing liquid in 2.5 pt. (1.5 l) of water and mix with the rhubarb extract.

Slugs

These slimy critters may cause damage in early spring when lily shoots are pushing through the soil and when the stems start to grow. Damaged stems can prevent flowering that year so it's important to get rid of the slugs with traps or by laying pellets. Make sure the latter are pet friendly.

Red lily beetle

This insect spells serious trouble for lilies and it seems to be extending its territory. Once known primarily in Europe, in warmer areas, it has crossed to the Eastern United States and is a problem in eastern Canadian provinces. Recently it has been detected in Manitoba.

According to information published by the University of Rhode Island, it was first discovered in the United States in 1992 in Cambridge, Massachusetts. Red lily beetles are strong fliers and can also move from one area to another on host plants.

The pest lays its eggs on true lilies and *Fritillaria* species, although researchers in Rhode Island have found it feeding on other host plants including various hosta species. It does not attack daylilies.

The beetles are bright red, about 0.2 in. (6 mm) long and their larvae look like tiny slugs, repulsive to look at, because of their habit of piling their excrement on their backs as they feed. This may be effective but it is definitely an extreme defense in the battle against predators!

Both eat lily foliage and can strip a plant to bare stem in double-quick time. If you live in an area where the pest is common, keep a careful watch for it. If you try to remove the beetles or larvae by hand, make sure you place a container under where you are working, to catch them if they drop.

Adult females lay their eggs on the undersides of the foliage. The larval feeding period lasts for 16–24 days, and new adults emerge after pupation, 16–22 days later, and start the destructive feeding all over again.

An unnamed Orienpet seedling

Some gardeners report success using Neem products to deal with the pest. Frequent applications may be necessary, starting early in the season. The adults overwinter in the soil or on leaf debris and can appear from late March if the weather is warm.

The North American Lily Society is devoting funds to investigate introducing predators of the beetle. There is a wasp that attacks the lily beetle specifically which, if introduced, may be an effective control. Although ordinary pesticides like bifenthrin (registered for U.S. use on greenhouse ornamentals) or Sevin, a carbamate, are protective, the real worry is for the native species. As Arthur Evans, a director of the research program, notes, no one keeps them sprayed, and the beetles love them.

Lily thrips

These miniscule black insects live out their entire life cycle in the bulb, often concentrating their munching near the bases of the scales. Bulbs weaken, disease follows and the bulbs rot away.

Soaking the bulbs in hot water – 111°F (44°C) – for an hour will kill the thrips. Dipping the bulbs in an insecticide solution – acephate or malathion – is also effective.

Weevils

Weevils are small beetles with snouts. They come out at night and can cause damage to plants in different ways. Most visible are the notches eaten out of the sides of leaves by adult weevils. But it is their larvae that tend to cause more damage to lilies. Small, white, half-moon-shaped grubs with brown heads, they feed on the bulbs and roots, often of containerized lilies, or they will chew around the stem of the plant just at or below the surface of the soil, which kills the plant by preventing water from moving up the stem. You may be unaware of their presence in the soil until, quite suddenly, the plant wilts and quickly dies.

Adults first appear in mid to late spring. Females live from five to 12 months and can lay up to 1,000 eggs, of which approximately half will develop. They overwinter both as larvae and adults.

Systemic insecticides are effective in controlling them. Garlic planted nearby may repel them or they can be shaken off the plants onto newspaper or burlap placed on the ground. Ground beetles are predators to weevils.

Virus disease

Some lilies are more prone to virus attack than others. *Lilium lancifolium* is an example, although it is reputed to live happily, even though affected, without showing any symptoms; the danger is that it will pass on the disease to other species or varieties. *L. candidum* and *L. longiflorum* are other species susceptible to virus infection.

It is a good idea to separate tulips from lilies in the garden, as they also are notorious virus carriers. Conifers or shrubs make good barriers.

Asiatic 'Sunshine Yellow'

Symptoms of virus disease are varied. Leaves can be mottled, flecked or curled; flower production can be affected with a decrease in numbers over a couple of seasons; flowers may be smaller and the plant gradually deteriorates. Flowers may show "breaking," the famous effect of striping of the flower's color that was a mark of the tulips sought after in 17th-century Holland. In some cases the bulbs are marked with brown rings.

There is no cure for virus disease. The only solution is to dig up the affected bulbs and, preferably, burn them. Any propagating from the bulbs, bulbils, scales or bulblets of infected plants will carry the virus over into new plants. However, new plants established from seed – even seed of infected plants – will avoid the virus. So accepting seed from a generous lily-growing friend is much safer than accepting bulbs.

Edward McRae notes in *Lilies, A Guide for Growers and Collectors* that many Trumpet, Aurelian and Oriental cultivars are tolerant of virus. He is adamant that hybridizers should always select one parent with a high degree of virus tolerance when breeding new cultivars.

Following is a short list of virus-resistant lily hybrids that have been in cultivation for many years:

'Connecticut King', 'Connecticut Lemonglow', 'Gold Eagle', 'Journey's End', 'Paprika', 'Piedmont', 'Shooting Star', 'Sunray', 'Tabasco', 'Thunderbolt', 'Uchida' and 'White Henryi'.

The three best-known viruses that attack lilies are detailed below:

Tulip-breaking virus
One of the oldest viruses to follow in the footsteps of gardeners, this one is virulent. It announces its presence with streaking or blotching on the buds, and the petals of opened flowers show dark streaks.

Cucumber mosaic virus
This widespread disease affects many plants as well as lilies. Leaves become malformed and brittle, foliage color may be very streaked and plants are stunted.

Lily symptomless virus
As the name implies, this one is harder to detect. It weakens the plant generally, can cause stunting and the plant gradually dies, often helped on its way by other diseases that attack a weak plant.

Fungus disease
Basal rot
This disease is recognized by a dark brown rot extending into the scales from the base of the bulb and is characterized by the roots dying. As the bulb degenerates the foliage yellows and the plant collapses. It is caused by the presence of *fusarium oxysporum*, a fungus disease in the soil, which seems to be most serious where lily bulbs live in warm, moist soil and tends therefore to be a problem of late summer.

Of course, the plants need water to grow and flower but the problem can be eased if irrigation is applied to the lower surface of the soil (perhaps by means of a buried dripper hose). The basal roots will absorb it and the bulb itself is able to rest in dry soil. Plants that have established a vigorous network

Asiatic 'Mirage'

of roots and where the bulbs are living in well-fertilized, friable soil will best be able to profit from this system. As an extra measure of protection the bulbs can be surrounded by coarse sand, which allows moisture to drain away from them. The soil will still retain heat, but not moist heat.

During warm summers avoid overwatering. In fact, lilies can survive without frequent irrigation.

If you detect basal rot early enough, you may be able to stop it in its tracks by lifting the bulb and standing it in a mixture of household bleach and water – one teaspoonful of bleach to a cup of water – or a fungicide for half an hour. And don't forget to lift and check nearby bulbs in case the disease has spread. Any badly infected bulbs should be destroyed.

Check out any new bulbs before planting to make sure they are clean.

Botrytis elliptica

This is another fungus disease that frequently attacks lilies, but it's not fatal and is usually caused by specific conditions. It often follows a wet spring. Overwatering can also bring it on. The first signs of *botrytis* may be white spots on the leaves that gradually increase in size causing the leaf to go brown, wither

and die. Typically, the infection starts at the bottom of the plant and moves up progressively. Flowers can also be affected and in severe cases the disease enters the stem and the whole plant collapses. The bulb is usually not affected and the following year, given the right conditions, the plants will again produce healthy flowers.

Moisture is necessary for the disease to develop and it may take only 24 hours of wet summer weather to cause a devastating outbreak. *Botrytis* is spread by spores; any injured tissue on the plant is an invitation to these spores to settle in and get to work, but the disease can be checked by spraying if it is noticed before it becomes too serious. The foliage must be dry and it is important to treat the undersides of the leaves where the spores first develop.

Bordeaux mixture (containing lime, copper sulphate, water and a fixing agent) and Kocide, another copper-based spray, are both effective.

The fungus overwinters in decaying organic matter so it is imperative to clean up thoroughly in the fall in affected areas. If possible, burn the detritus; on no account add it to the compost heap.

Good air circulation helps to prevent its onset. In dry, cold climates it is rarely a problem.

Disorders

Fasciation

This is a somewhat intriguing deformation of the plant that usually causes flattening and squaring of the stem and occasionally a hugely increased number of flowers, often in very close formation. It is thought that it may be caused by a sudden change in growing conditions from the previous season, although it seems some cultivars are genetically prone to the disorder. The lily will revert to its normal form the following year.

Yellow or chlorotic foliage

This may occur where the soil is very chalky or limy. It can be corrected by reducing the pH of the soil and/or spraying with a chelated iron compound.

Lilies in Cold Climates

The following personal observations come from Lynnette Westfall of Valley K Greenhouses in Edberg, Alberta. Lilies are Lynnette's passion as well as her business, and her experience of growing both hybrids and species is of value to lily enthusiasts in cold climates. Lilies are increasingly popular in cold climates and interest in the genus is growing fast. Many growers are prepared to take special precautions to ensure that their precious bulbs survive the winter.

Our climate is quite harsh (zone 3) and we have experienced many winters without reliable snow for protection in the past five to 10 years. Even a couple of inches of snow provides good protection, and a foot of snow is great! We have been having periods of drought for the last three years as well; the summer of 2002 was the worst on record in 133 years in Alberta. Our springs are unpredictable – one day may be 50°F (10°C), then the next day 5°F (-15°C). Killing and damaging frosts occur often after the lilies have pushed their noses through the ground. We can still experience killing frosts in mid-June in central Alberta.

Our lilies start to push through the ground as early as the beginning of April during a warm spring. The average date for emergence here is the end of April, although in the spring of 2002 (very, very cold), they did not emerge until after May 20th. Extreme heat by the end of June allowed them to catch up and bloom only one to two weeks off their regular bloom period, but the bulb health suffered as a result of the rapid top growth. Most notably, the root systems on newly planted bulbs (fall 2001 and spring 2002) were underdeveloped or nonexistent. During harvest in fall, it was quite surprising to find inadequate and nonexistent roots under bulbs that bloomed beautifully during summer. It was very disheartening to realize that bulbs without adequate roots prior to the onset of winter would likely not survive the winter or another dry spring.

I have found the established LA hybrids to be virtually unaffected by drought, while young seedlings seem to struggle in early spring without adequate moisture. The LAs appear to be perfectly hardy without any protection here at our zone 3 location, but we have customers in Calgary (chinook territory, zones 3–4) who cannot overwinter them. Zone 2 growers (Vermilion, Alberta) also have no luck with overwintering them.

Our Asiatic selections have been affected by drought and heat most notably in their height and colors. The colors have shown quite a variance over the past three years, depending on the heat factor when they first open. Hot temperatures wash the colors out, while cool temperatures make for more vivid colors.

Often I have wondered if I had certain varieties tagged incorrectly as the flower colors did not resemble the previous year's colors at all. Typically the lilies only achieve two-thirds or half their height potential under drought conditions. Hardiness of Asiatics does not seem to be affected by drought or lack of snow cover over winter. They are truly hardy! Only those stressed or affected by disease such as *fusarium* or basal rot struggle to survive our harsh winters.

With all varieties of lilies, their ability to increase in bulb size has been affected by drought conditions – they do not gain any size from the previous year if they do not receive adequate moisture. They have also started to reproduce themselves much more prolifically these last two years in an effort to overcome the stresses Mother Nature inflicts on them. This is a common

Lilium martagon

occurrence in many plants – to reproduce themselves when they feel their existence is threatened.

The LA hybrids tend to reproduce prolifically under normal growing conditions, but have kicked into overdrive with the weather patterns of the last two years! It is not uncommon to find many underground bulblets the size of a nickel or bigger when harvesting mature LA hybrid bulbs. These bulblets try to bloom their second year, but we pinch the buds off as soon as they begin to form, in order to allow the bulb to use the energy to increase in size rather than expending itself in immature blooms.

LAs also double their original bulb size under good growing conditions. I have heard some say they are not long-lived, but with prolific reproduction the mother bulbs do not need to be. There is one drawback I find with the LA hybrids, and that is their virus resistance, or lack of it. I find that many varieties succumb to tulip-breaking virus over time, usually three to five years, and it will appear if present. It is worth noting that I have never seen virus in any of the Royal series of LA hybrids. It is my personal theory that the interdivisional crosses (which the LAs are) are genetically weaker because of the cross, and this makes them more susceptible to virus. Stress triggers the virus, and of course our unpredictable and harsh climate puts them under stress, so we have seen more virus symptoms in the past two years than ever before.

We promptly remove and burn stock suspected of being infected with virus, so it won't spread to other varieties.

What have we done to help them overcome the stresses of weather? Mulch, mulch and more mulch! Mulch is effective in controlling ground temperature, moisture levels, pests and soil-borne diseases. Mulch spread throughout the beds to a depth of even 2 in. (5 cm) is very beneficial in keeping moisture in the ground – I cannot stress this enough! I would recommend mulch to a depth of at least 4 in. (10 cm) wherever possible, but any depth is better than none at all. Mulch also provides extra winter protection during years without snow cover.

I highly recommend applying mulch over varieties that are under particular stress, or less hardy (such as Orienpets and Orientals), to a depth of 6–8 in. (15–20 cm) for winter. Mulch also is effective in keeping the ground temperature consistent in spring, and slowing the thawing process so that the lilies will emerge a little later than those without mulch, and perhaps escape the late killing frosts as a result. Slow and steady ground temperatures encourage good root systems to develop before top growth begins.

We use bark mulch throughout our lily beds, and have used dried grass clippings and sawdust in the past as well.

We are fortunate to have a variety of soil conditions throughout our small acreage – we live within quarter of a mile of a large river valley; almost pure sand to healthy, rich black soil exists here. The lilies do the best in the sandy areas, providing they receive adequate moisture. If not, the lilies in these areas are the first to suffer under drought.

The most common reason for bulb rot in containers, however, is too much moisture and not enough drainage. It is worth noting that heavy additions of sand to the potting mix used in containers makes for much fatter and healthier bulbs by the time fall rolls around. If soil structure contains a high ratio of sand, extra fertilizing will be needed.

We do not grow Orientals or Trumpets in the ground here at our location due to their lack of reliable hardiness. We grow them in containers over summer, harvest in fall and store in a ground cold pit at 35°F (2°C) over winter. We live in the country, where temperatures plunge a little bit fur-

Oriental seedling

ther than in the towns or cities. We do have many customers who live within towns or cities who have great success with overwintering their Orientals and Trumpets in zone 3, when planted against heated foundations or protected sites. The common complaint is that they still do not thrive, bud count decreases each year and they eventually die out, usually within three years of planting.

The latest in interdivisional crosses (Orienpets, Asiapets and Asiatic/Aurelian crosses) have given us mixed results over the past four years. We find those bred on the prairies grow best on the prairies, such as Wilbert Ronald and Lynn Collicut's selections ('Northern Star', 'Northern Carillon', 'Starburst Sensation', 'Easter Morn', etc.). 'Scheherazade' and 'Leslie Woodriff' (both Orienpets bred outside of Canada) have proven reliably hardy here as well, providing they are planted at a minimum depth of 8 in. (20 cm), and planted in spring so as to allow good root growth over summer, prior to the onset of winter. Most Orienpets are doing very well in provinces such as Manitoba where they still get good snow cover over winter, but here in Alberta mixed results are found when we have no snow cover. Again, we recommend planting these in spring only, to a depth of 8–12 in. (20–30 cm), and heavy mulching in fall before snow falls. The mulch must be removed as soon as possible in spring, in order for the bulb to warm up and start growing. Because they are planted deeper, they will take longer to emerge. The alternative is to grow them in containers and overwinter in a protected spot or root cellar.

My biggest concern with the hardiness of the Orienpets and Orientals revolves around their late blooming natures. We experience killing frosts as early as mid-August, which is often the time the buds are just maturing on these varieties here. If they freeze hard too early in their life cycle, the bulb is unable to gather enough energy before winter sets in, and this may very well be the reason they do not survive the winter extremes on the prairies. I believe they have the ability to still collect some energy through the stems even after they are limp after a killing frost, so we leave those ugly frozen stems on them despite their unsightly appearance.

We fertilize by adding a slow release pellet (14-14-14 – three to four month life) in early spring, as soon as the lilies emerge. This is scratched into the ground just below the surface of each clump or row. We use a water-soluble fertilizer of 15-30-15 during irrigation once, just prior to buds opening, and we also use a water-soluble fertilizer of 20-18-18 with minor trace elements added once during the growing season, shortly after flowering. It is only in the last two years that we have irrigated our lilies because of extreme drought conditions. Lilies are very drought tolerant providing they are healthy to begin with.

Disease is almost nonexistent here, probably due to the weather extremes. If we experience prolonged periods of cloudy, damp or wet weather, there is usually an outbreak of *botrytis* to follow, but it is easily controlled with a spray of Benomyl (severe outbreaks) every two weeks, or a simple baking-soda solution sprayed every three to four days as a preventative measure. It is worth noting that you can virtually guarantee *botrytis* will appear sooner or later if severe frosts occur during the early development of stems. Generous spacing of the bulbs goes a long way in controlling *botrytis* symptoms as well, as do good cleanup practices in fall. If we experience heavy *botrytis* during summer we pull the stems and burn them all in fall, otherwise we leave them over winter in order to trap more snow, and pull them in spring before the new shoots emerge.

Lilies are rarely affected by pests other than aphids at our location. I have never seen an outbreak in the lilies grown in the ground, but often they affect the containerized lilies. We control them very effectively with an organic product called End All, from Safer's.

The last two years have seen an increase in the grasshopper population, no doubt due to our drought and extreme heat. They have not damaged the lilies yet, presumably because they do not like the rough nature of the bark mulch that surrounds our lilies. Clouds of grasshoppers greeted us as we walked across the lawn in summer this year, but very few were found among the lily beds.

We grow a few lily species here with success: *Lilium cernuum*, *L. pumilum*, *L. citronella*, *L. lankongense*, *L. henryi*, *L. tsingtuaense* and, of course, *L. lancifolium*. We are experimenting with a great variety of others, but it is too soon to tell if they are reliably hardy under our conditions yet. We must evaluate their ability to thrive and reproduce, not just their ability to live under our conditions.

Martagons are extremely hardy lilies, but I only grow them in my personal collection, not for commercial use.

We split and divide our bulbs every three years on average, in order to prevent bulb deterioration due to overcrowding. Experience has shown us that if we leave them one extra year, we will end up digging and moving the entire row completely because the bulbs will deteriorate that quickly. Because we are commercial growers with the intent to ship the largest, healthiest bulbs possible, we snip the buds on immature stems, and cut off spent flowers immediately after blooming, to encourage the bulbs to put their energies into increasing bulb size rather than seed production.

Harvest is begun as soon as the stems begin to yellow and die off in fall; sometimes this is the end of August, sometimes not till the end of September. Stem ripening is greatly affected by the moisture levels in the ground; lots of moisture means they will be slower to ripen, less means they are quicker to ripen. If a stem does not tug out of the bulb easily or cleanly in one quick snap, then it is not ready to be harvested and we put them back in the ground and try again two weeks later. If a bulb is harvested too soon, its ability to survive and thrive the next year is affected. Flower and stem performance is directly linked to the growing conditions and treatment of the bulb the year before. Good growing practices this year result in great performance the next year.

APPENDIX II

Sources of Lily Bulbs and Information

The importation of live plants and plant materials across borders requires special arrangements, which will be detailed in suppliers' catalogs. Americans must have a permit, obtained through the website given below. Every order requires a phytosanitary certificate supplied by the exporter, and purchasers should verify this at the time of order. (If certain plants are exempt from this certificate, the seller will know.) A CITES (Convention on International Trade in Endangered Species of Wild Fauna and Flora) certificate may also be required if the plant is an endangered species. For more information contact:

USDA-APHIS-PPQ
Permit Unit
4700 River Road, Unit 136
Riverdale, MD 20727-1236
Ph: (301) 734-8645. Fax: (301) 734-5786
www.aphis.usda.gov

Canadians importing plant material must pay a fee and complete an "application for permit to import." A phytosanitary certificate may also be required. For more information contact:

Plant Health and Production Division
Canadian Food Inspection Agency
2nd Floor West, Permit Office
59 Camelot Drive
Nepean, ON K1A 0Y9
Ph: (613) 225-2342. Fax: (613) 228-6605
www.inspection.gc.ca

United States

Arrowhead Alpines
P.O. Box 857, Fowlerville, MI 48836
Ph: (517) 223-3581. Fax: (517) 223-8750

B & D Lilies
P.O. Box 2007, Port Townsend,
  WA 98368
Ph: (360) 385-1738
Website: www.bdlilies.com

Borbeleta Gardens, Inc.
15980 Canby Ave.
Faribault, MN 55021-7652
Ph: (507) 334-2807. Fax: (507) 334-0365

Hallson Gardens
411 Wolf Lake Dr., Brooklyn MI 49230
Ph: (517) 467-7955
E-mail: hallson@perennialnursery.com

Heronswood Nursery
7530 NE 288th St.
Kensington, WA 98346-9502
Ph: (360) 287-4172
Website: www.heronswood.com

The Lily Garden
4902 NE 147th Ave.
Vancouver, WA 98682-6067
Ph: (360) 253-6273
E-mail: Thelilygdn@aol.com

Maple Leaf Nursery
4236 Greenstone Rd.
Placerville, CA 95667
Ph: (530) 626-8371
E-mail: Maple_lf@inforum.net

McClure & Zimmerman
P.O. Box 368, Friesland, WI 53935-0368
Ph: (800) 883-6998
E-mail: Infor@mzbulb.com

Milaeger's Gardens
4838 Douglas Ave.
Racine, WI 53935-2498
Ph: (800) 669-9956

Old House Gardens
536 Third St.
Ann Arbor, MI 48103-4957
Ph: (734) 995-1486
E-mail: OHGBulbs@aol.com

Canada

Estate Perennials
Box 3683, Spruce Grove, AB T7X 3A9
Ph: (780) 963-7307
E-mail: Rfrey@hollandiabulbs.ca
Website: www.hollandiabulbs.ca

Hillcrest Harmony Flowers
Box 24, Churchbridge, SK S0A 0M0
Ph: (306) 896-2992

Jeffries Nurseries
Box 402
Portage la Prairie, MB RIN 3B7
Ph: (888) 857-5288. Fax: (204) 857-2877
Website: www.jeffriesnurseries.com

The Lily Nook
P.O. Box 846, Neepawa, MB R0J 1H0
Ph: (204) 476-3225
E-mail: Lilynook@mail.techplus.com

Thimble Farms
175 Arbutus Rd.
Salt Spring Island, BC V8K 1A3
Ph: (250) 537-5788

Valley K Greenhouses
RR 1, Edberg, AB T0B 1J0
Ph: (780) 877-2547. Fax: (780) 877-2540
Website: www.valleyk.com

Lily societies

North American Lily Society Inc.
P.O. Box 272
Owatonna, MN 55060
Website: www.lilies.org
The North American Lily Society lists a number of regional societies on its website.

New Zealand Lily Society
PO Box 1394
Christchurch
(This is the oldest Lily Society in the world. It celebrated its 70th anniversary in 2002.)

Species Lily Preservation Group
Mrs. Mary Barber
Membership Chair
336 Sandlewood Rd.
Oakville, ON L6L 3R8

The RHS Lily Group
The Royal Horticultural Society
80 Vincent Square
London SW1P2PE
E-mail: advisory@rhs.org.uk
Website: www.rhs.org.uk
Open by subscription to all Royal Horticultural Society members.

The International Lily Register

The ILR maintains a register of names for lily cultivars and cultivar groups. Anyone raising new cultivars is encouraged to register them. This is a free service through the Royal Horticultural Society that aims to avoid duplication of names or other confusion within the genus. The full Register, which contains details of raisers, parentage and classification, was published in 1982; since then regular supplements have brought it up to date.

Bibliography

Campbell-Culver, Maggie. *The Origin of Plants*. London: Headline, 2001

Coats, Peter. *Flowers in History*. London: Wiedenfeld and Nicolson, 1970

Consider the Lilies. New York: W. & E. Marshall & Co., Inc., 1928

Fox, Derek. *Lilies – A Wisley Handbook*. London. The Royal Horticultural Society, 1985

Hobbs, Jack and Hatch, Terry. *Bulbs for New Zealand Gardeners and Collectors*. Auckland: Godwit, 1994

Jefferson-Brown, M. J. *Modern Lilies*. London: Faber and Faber, 1965

Jefferson-Brown, Michael and Howland, Harris. *The Gardener's Guide to Growing Lilies*. Devon: David & Charles Publishers, 1995

Lilies and Related Plants. London: The Royal Horticultural Society Lily Group, 1988–9

Lilies and Related Plants. London: The Royal Horticultural Society Lily Group, Supplement, 1990

Lilies and Related Plants. London: The Royal Horticultural Society Lily Group, 1992

The Lily Year Book, London. The Royal Horticultural Society, 1957

McArthur, Glad. *Glad McArthur's Lifetime of Gardening*. Dunedin: John McIndoe Ltd., 1992

McRae, Edward Austin. *Lilies, A Guide for Growers and Collectors*. Portland: Timber Press, 1998

Thomas, Graham Stuart. *New Edition Perennial Garden Plants or The Modern Florilegium*. London: J.M. Dent & Sons Ltd. in association with the RHS, 1982

Index